Contemporary Theory Primer

by Margaret Brandman

A Companion Workbook to:

Contemporary Piano Method - Junior Primer & Book 1A
&
Playing Made Easy for Recorder

Exclusive Distributors for Australia and New Zealand
Encore Music Distributors
227 Napier St. Fitzroy. 3065 Victoria Australia
Ph +61 3 9415 6677
Facsimile +61 3 9415 6655
Email: sales@encoremusic.com.au

This book © Copyright 2015 by Margaret Brandman trading as Jazzem Music
46 Gerrale St, Cronulla NSW 2230 Australia
ISBN 978-949683-23-6
Order Number MMP 8020
International copyright secured (APRA/AMCOS). All rights reserved.

Unauthorised reproduction of any part
of this publication by any means including
photocopying is an infringement of copyright.

Introduction

The objective of the material presented in this Preparatory Level of the Contemporary Theory Workbook series is to develop fluency in two vital areas of music study.

1) Interval and pattern reading - via the simplified interval approach
2) Rhythm reading and performance skills with a variety of note values and varying time signatures

Facility in these areas is the key to top performers' ability to sight read and learn music quickly and easily.

Several accelerated learning techniques are employed to achieve this fluency — namely Spatial Orientation, Pattern Recognition and Colour. In addition the use of touch, as in the act of colouring in, brings in yet another sense to solidify the student's understanding of the topic. Refer to the outside back of this book for a full colour sample of the colour boxes. For more information on the methodology read the introduction to the Contemporary Piano Method - Book 1A or the Junior Primer.

This book can be used as a stand-alone theory book or to complement the following practical materials:-
1) Contemporary Piano Method - Junior Primer and Book 1A (and related supplementary materials *)
2) Playing Made Easy for Recorder
3) Contemporary Aural Course - Preparatory Level, Set One and Set Two

To continue interval learning and to move on to other standard theory topics, follow this book with Contemporary Theory Workbook - Book 1.

Dr. Margaret Brandman
Ph.D (Mus/Arts)., HonDL (IBC)., B.Mus.(Comp).,
T.Mus.A., HonFNMSM.., F.Comp.ASMC., L.Perf.ASMC.,
F.Mus.Ed.ASMC., DipE.WPTA., A.Mus.A., A.S.A T.Dip

* **Related Supplementary Material**
  - Contemporary Piano Method –DVD
  - Geometry of the Piano –DVD
  - Daily Dexter-Flexers
  - Dexter's Easy Piano Pieces
  - Junior Trax

Contents

Keyboard Signpost Keys 4
Keyboard Quiz 5
Staff Notation 6
Sounds 7
Intervals - Same, Step and Skip 8
Interval Quiz 9
Keyboard Pictures of Three Easy Intervals 10
Interval Quiz 11
Rhythm in Music 12
Rhythm Quiz 13
Colour and Clap - Colour Chart 14
Rhythm Activities 15
The Great Staff 16
How Well Do You Know Your Cs 17
Another interval - Skip Plus One 18
Writing Intervals 19
Rhythm Activities 20
Search and Rescue 21
Interval Quiz 22
Rhythm Activities 23
Writing Interval Sets 24
Rhythm Activities 25
The Root Position Triad 26-27
Rhythm Activities 28
Leger Lines 29
Rhythm Activities - Odd Times 30
Stems 31
Pitch Chart and Signpost Cs 32
Writing Music with Whole Notes 33
Writing Music with Half Notes 34
Writing Music with Quarter Notes 35
Larger Intervals: Sixths, Sevenths and Octaves 36
Activities 37
Interval Overview - Unison to Octave 38
Interval Family Quiz 39
Speed Music Reading Quiz 40

KEYBOARD SIGNPOST KEYS

C is to the **left** of the group of **two** black keys

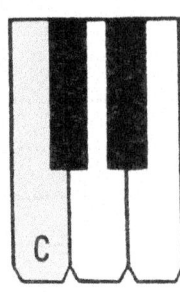

F is to the **left** of the group of **three** black keys

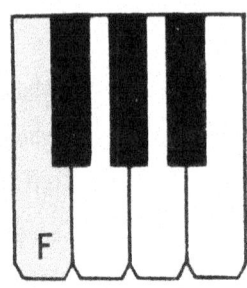

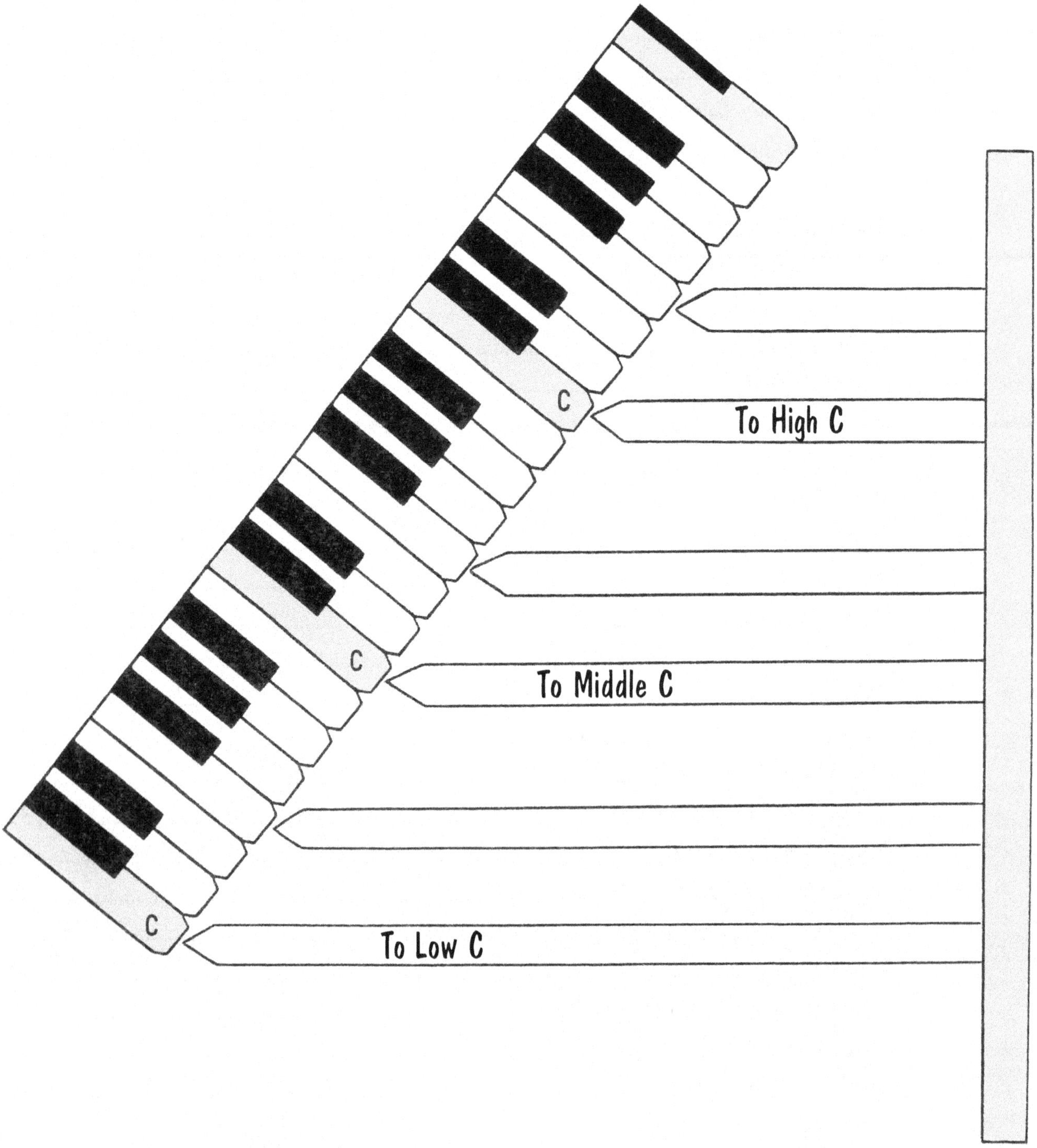

To High C

To Middle C

To Low C

KEYBOARD QUIZ 5

In music we only use seven alphabet letter names: A B C D E F G
Notice how they appear several times on the keyboard.

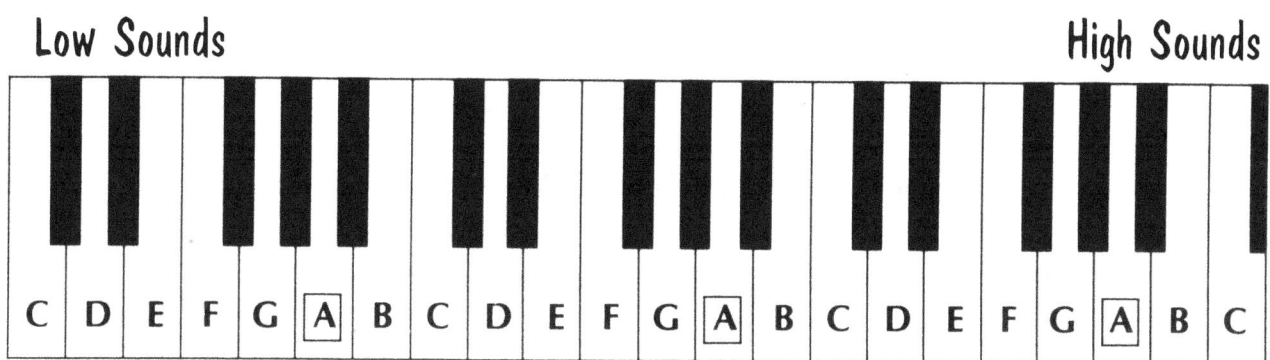

1) Keyboard Signpost Search.
   Colour all the Cs in RED pencil. Colour all the Fs in GREEN.

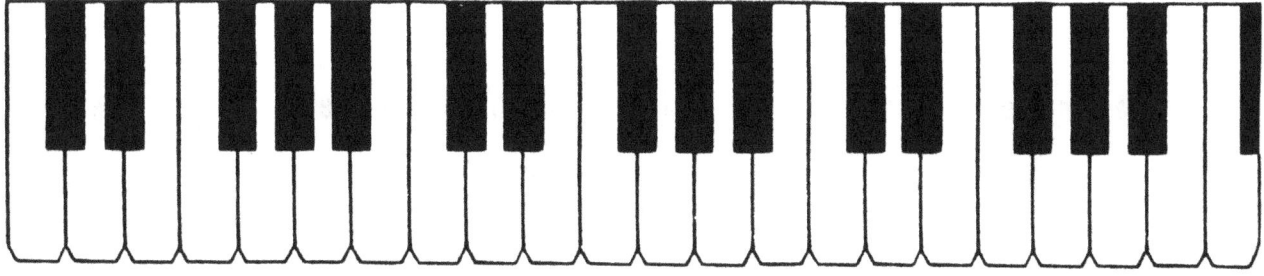

2) Keyboard Name Game.
   Write the names on the keys that the arrows point to.

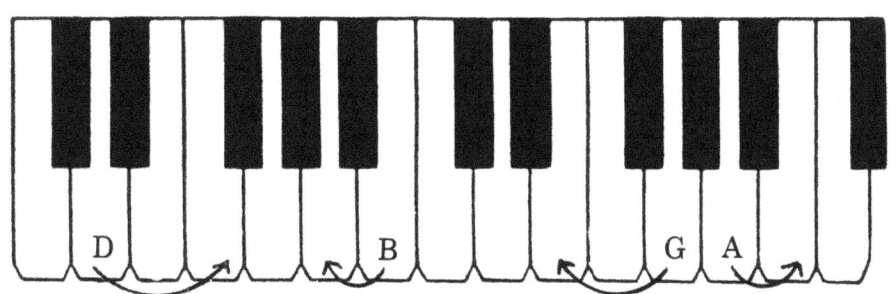

STAFF NOTATION

The **Staff** or **Stave** is the set of **five lines** and **four spaces** on which music is written.

A STAFF

The lines and spaces are numbered from bottom to top.

Line Note

The note goes around the line

Space Note

The note is in-between two lines

Space notes can also be written on top of the fifth line or below the first line

Extra lines for musical sounds

Leger Lines

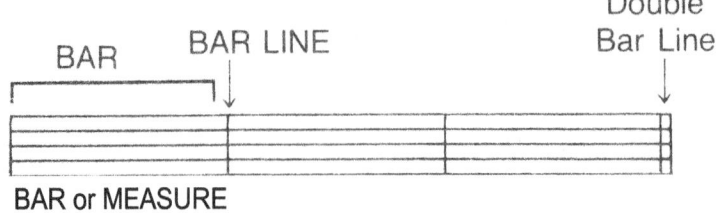

Single Bar Lines

Upright lines are used to divide music into bars or measures

BAR   BAR LINE

BAR or MEASURE

Double Bar Line

Double Bar Lines

The double lines show the end of the music

SOUNDS ⑦

If a note is written high on the Staff it will sound HIGH ↑

If a note is written low on the Staff it will sound LOW ↓

Activities

1) Copy these notes on the staff

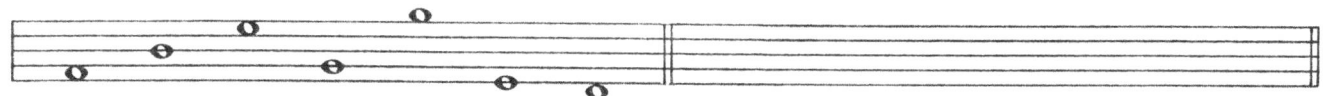

2) Identify these as Line Notes (L) or Space Notes (S)

3) Tick the HIGHEST note of each group

4) Tick the LOWEST note of each group

5) Draw some LINE notes on the staff lines and on Leger Lines

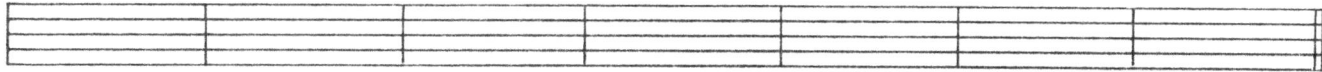

6) Draw some SPACE notes on the staff and on Leger Lines

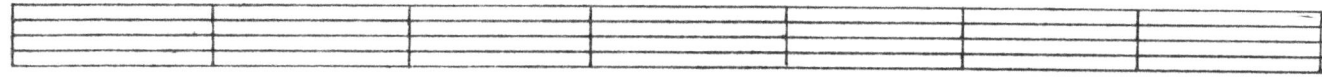

INTERVALS

An interval is the distance between two notes.
Each interval has its own special look on the staff, feel on the instrument and individual sound.

THE MUSIC LADDER OR STAIRCASE

When music is written on a staff using alternating lines and spaces the resulting look is that of a ladder.

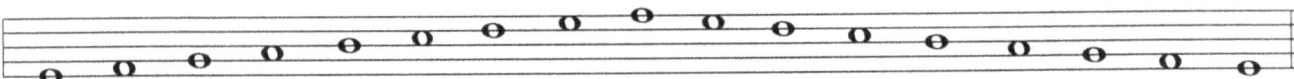

As notes move up on the ladder they have higher sounds and as they move down they sound lower.

Here are the first three intervals....

1) SAME or repeated note. The notes look the same, feel the same and sound the same.

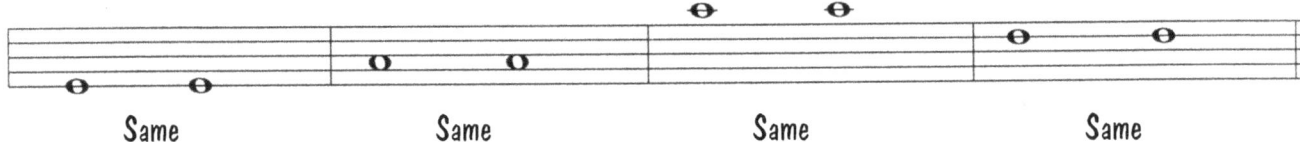

Same   Same   Same   Same

2) STEP This interval moves along the ladder from line note to space note, or vice versa.

Step Up	Step Up	Step Down	Step Down	Steps Up	Steps Down

Line Space   Space Line   L   S   S   L

3) SKIP This interval moves from line note to line note, or from space note to space note skipping over one of the notes in the music ladder.

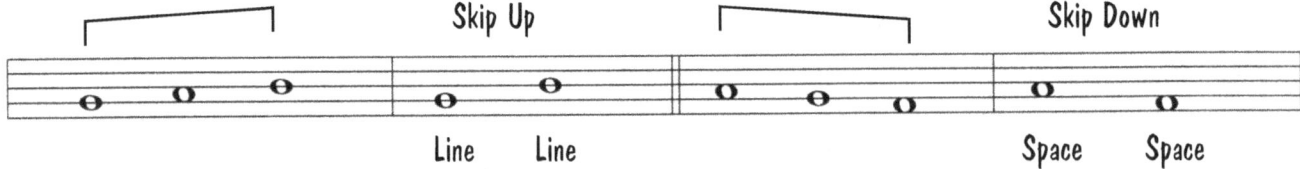

Skip Up   Skip Down

Line   Line   Space   Space

DIRECTION

Notes on one staff can move either up or down or remain the same.
Notes on two staves can be seen to move in various ways: same, up, down, out, in, oblique.

Up	Down	Out	In	Same	Oblique	OR	Oblique

INTERVAL QUIZ 9

PART A

1) Write some SAMES (repeated notes) alongside the given note.

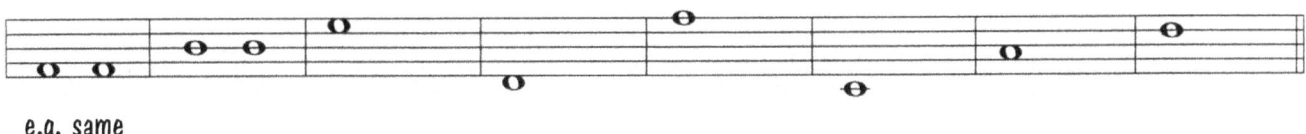

e.g. same

2. Write STEPS going up or down. Follow the arrows

e.g. step   ↑   ↑   ↑   ↓   ↓   ↓   ↑

3. Search and Rescue : Find the steps in this line of music and circle them

PART B

4. Write SKIPS moving up or down (from a line to the next line, or a space to the next space)

e.g. skip   ↑   ↑   ↑   ↓   ↓   ↓   ↓

5. Search and Rescue : Find the skips in this line of music and circle them

6. In which direction do the notes move for both parts? Up, Down, Out, In, or Same
   * first draw lines along the music
   * then draw matching lines from the music to the words, using a different colour pencil for each one

   (a) Out   (b) In   (c) Up   (d) Down   (e) Same

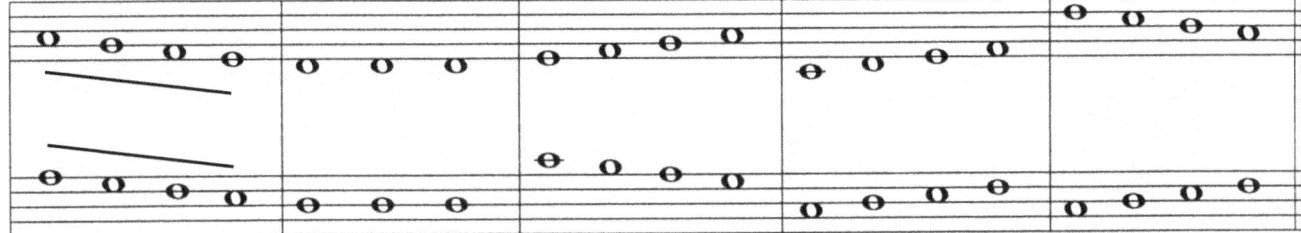

THREE EASY INTERVALS

Play and listen to these intervals in different areas of your instrument.
To play these on a keyboard, think of the notes as the ends of your fingertips, as if you had drawn a circle around each one.
Place your fingers on the notes drawn on this page to feel the distances.

Steps

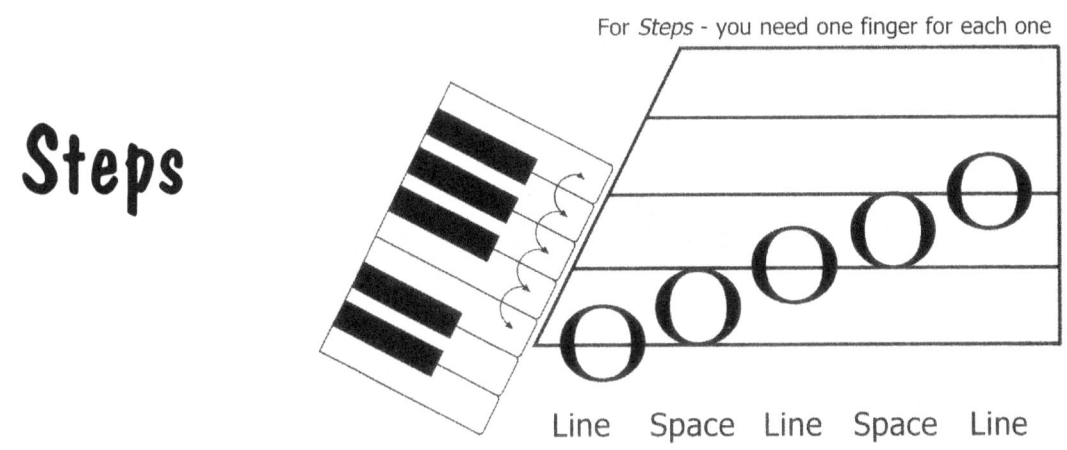

For *Steps* - you need one finger for each one

Line   Space   Line   Space   Line

Skips

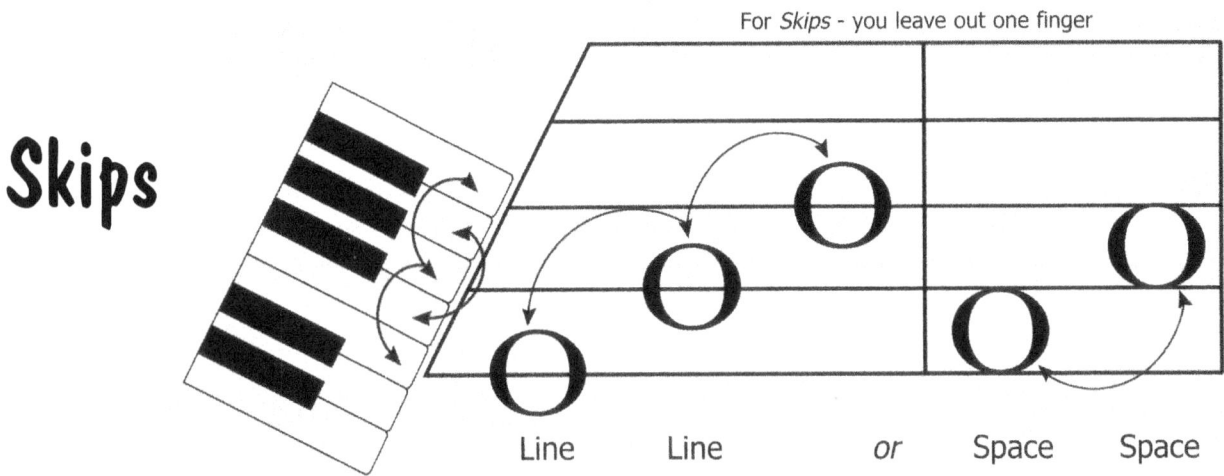

For *Skips* - you leave out one finger

Line   Line   *or*   Space   Space

Jumps

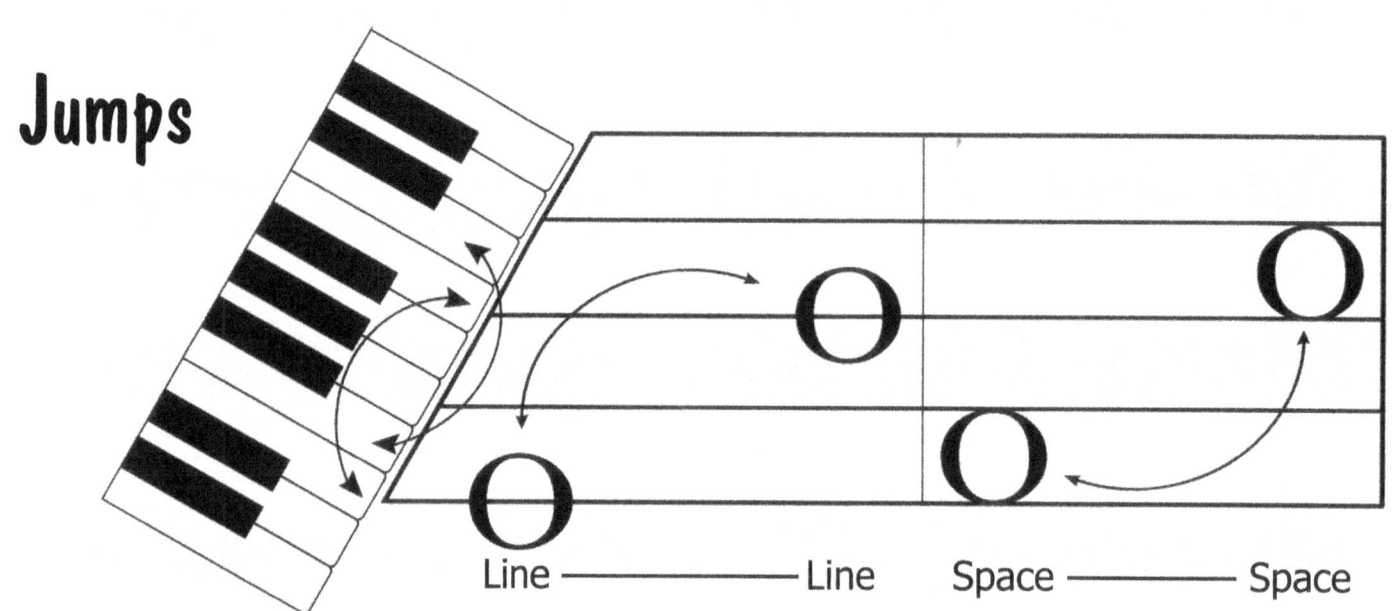

Line ——— Line   Space ——— Space

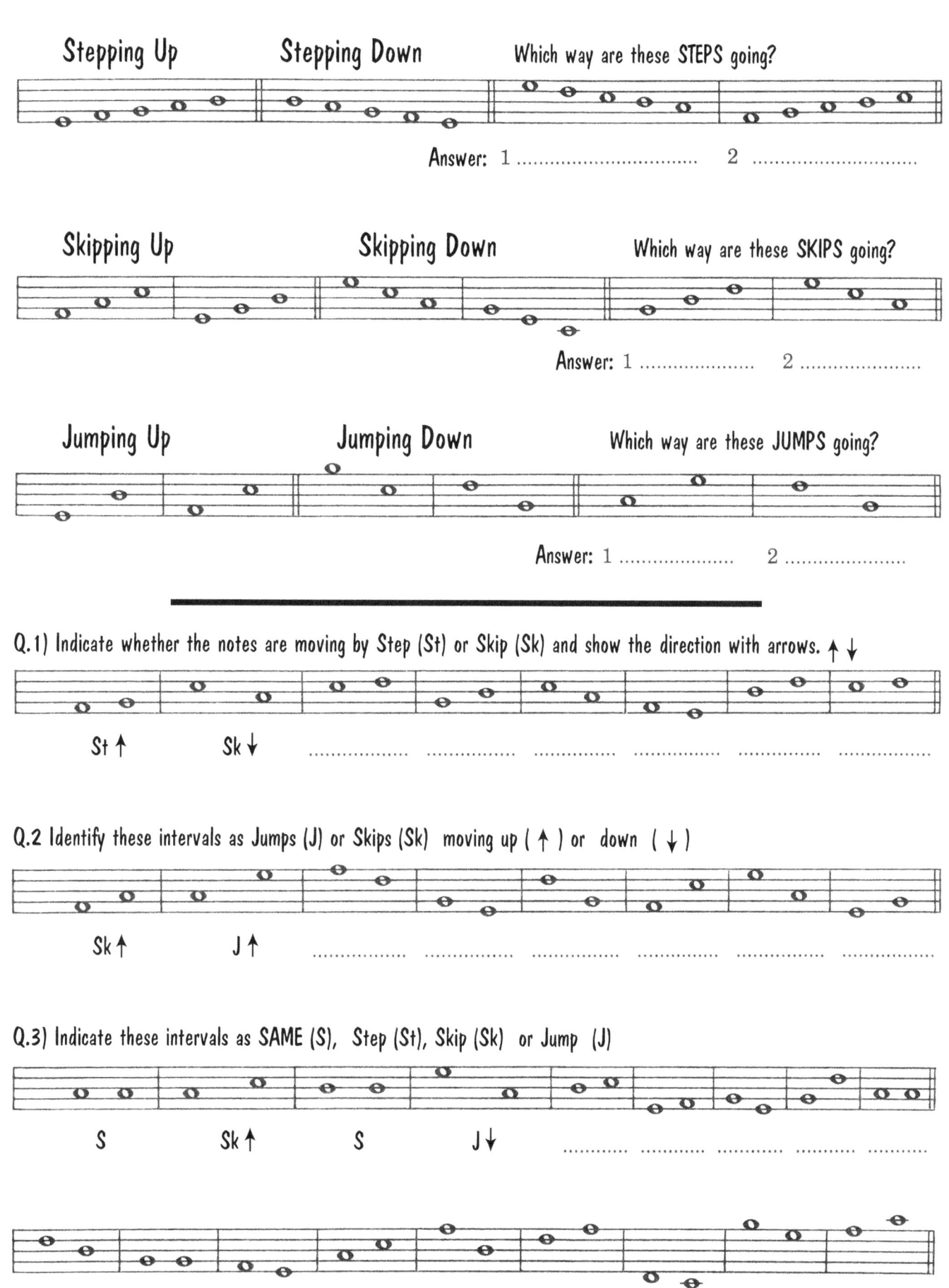

RHYTHM IN MUSIC

Notes

Notes can have different shapes to show how long each sound continues.

A note that lasts for **4 counts** looks like this: 𝅝

A note that lasts for **2 counts** looks like this: 𝅗𝅥 OR 𝅗𝅥

A note that lasts for **1 count** looks like this: ♩ OR ♩

The value names of the notes are as follows:

𝅝 - Whole Note or Semibreve

𝅗𝅥 - Half Note or Minim

♩ - Quarter Note or Crotchet

Rests

Rests are signs which indicate silence. Each type of note has a matching rest.

A Whole Rest or Semibreve Rest looks like this: ⟶ 4 counts

A Half Rest or Minim Rest looks like this: ⟶ 2 counts

A Quarter Rest or Crotchet Rest looks like this: ⟶ 1 count

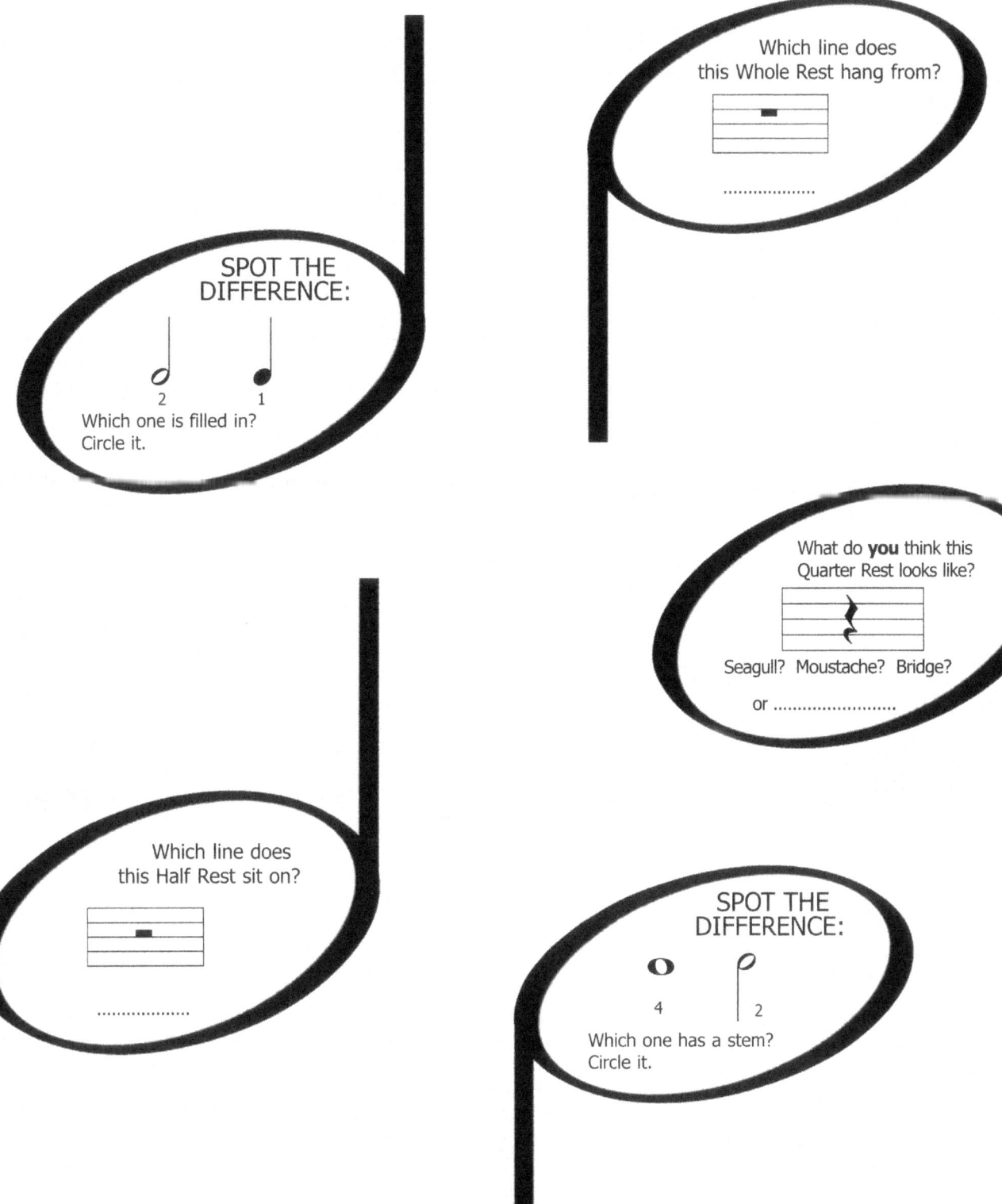

COLOUR AND CLAP - COLOUR CHART

NOTES: Play Clap or Sing.

Refer to the outside back of the Contemporary Piano Method -Junior Primer for a full colour sample of the top half of this page.

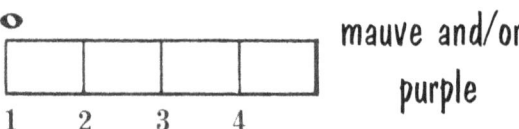 mauve and/or purple

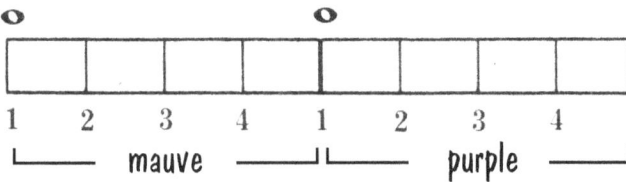

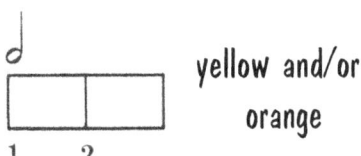 yellow and/or orange

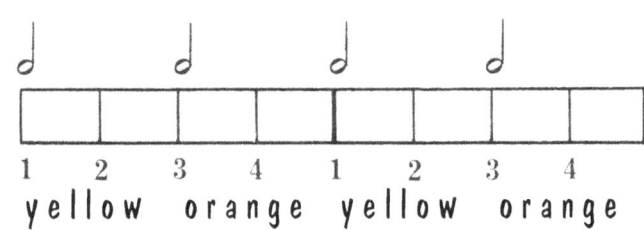

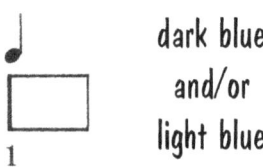 dark blue and/or light blue

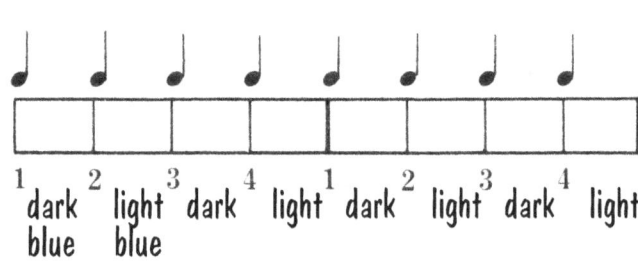

RESTS: Silence. Stop playing, clapping or singing, just keep counting

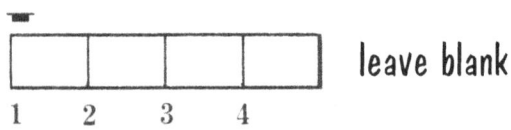 leave blank

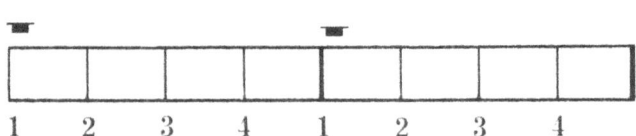

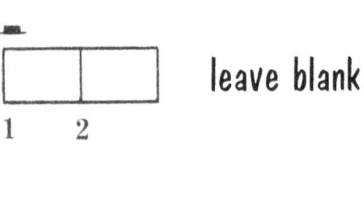 leave blank

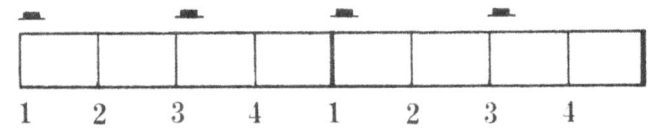

 leave blank

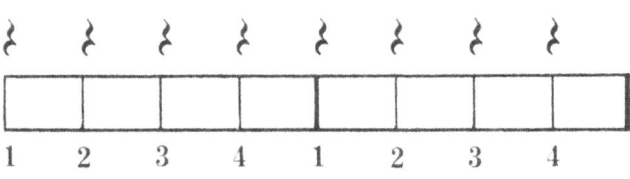

RHYTHM ACTIVITIES

Time Signature

$\frac{4}{4}$ The Time Signature (sign) consists of the two numbers at the beginning of the music.
The **top** number tells **how many** counts in the bar and the **lower** number tells **what kind** of note (for example half note (𝅗𝅥) or quarter note (♩) receives one count.
$\frac{4}{4}$ means four lots of 1/4 notes (blues) per bar.

Colouring, Counting and Clapping

The colouring and counting activities in this book all have the quarter note or crotchet as the beat note. Make sure you pay attention to the TOP number of each of the Time Signatures, so that you will know how many counts in each bar or measure.

Colour in the boxes and clap the time values

When clapping, hold your hands together while the colour continues and clap again when a new colour comes along. Takes hands apart and beat time in the air when a rest comes along.

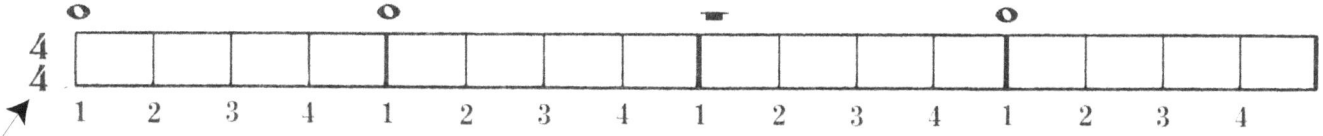

Highlight lower number in blue

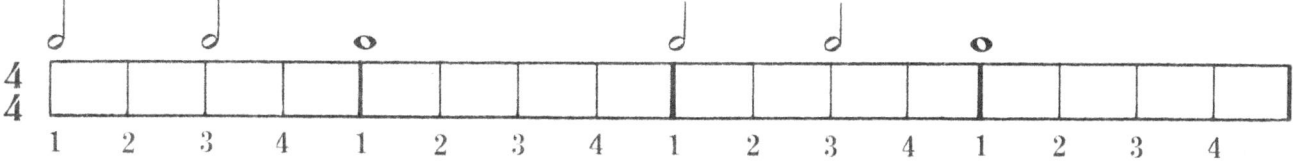

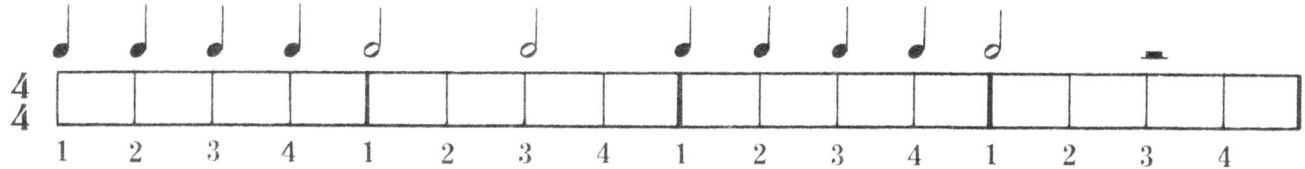

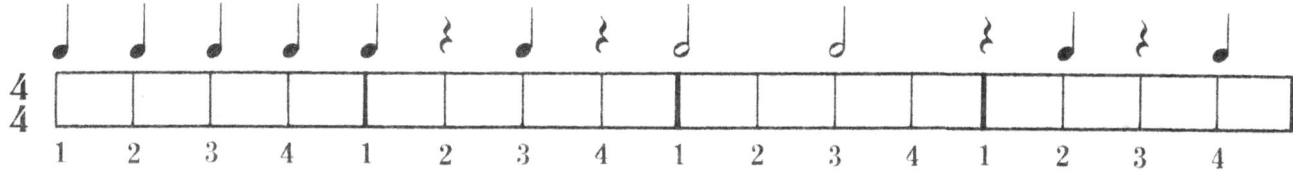

THE GREAT STAFF

The Great Staff is an eleven line staff made up of a Treble Staff and a Bass Staff plus the extra leger line for Middle C, all joined by a brace. It is also known as a Grand Staff.

Although the theoretical position for Middle C is exactly in the centre of the two staves, Middle C is written closer to the Treble Staff, to indicate that the Right Hand plays it on a keyboard and closer to the Bass Staff to indicate that it is played by the Left Hand on a keyboard.

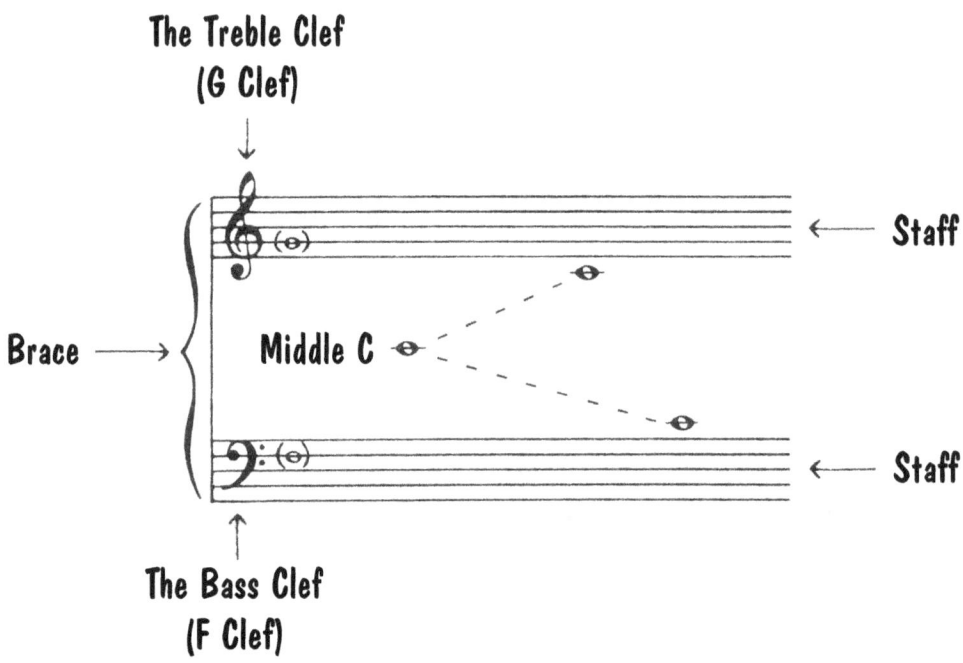

The Treble Clef  usually indicates that on a keyboard the Right Hand plays the notes on its staff. It is also known as the G Clef as it is a fancy or stylised letter G. The curl in the middle begins on the line that the note G is written on (2nd line)

The Bass Clef usually indicates that on a keyboard the Left Hand plays the notes on its staff. It is also known as the F Clef as it is a fancy or stylised letter F. The two dots surround the line that the note F is written on (4th line)

MEMORY POSITIONS FOR SIGNPOST Cs

Very High C - 2 leger lines above
High C - on Treble Clef's curl
Middle C - Line through ball

Middle C - Bass Clef's hat
Low C - Sits under the dots
Very Low C - 2 leger lines below

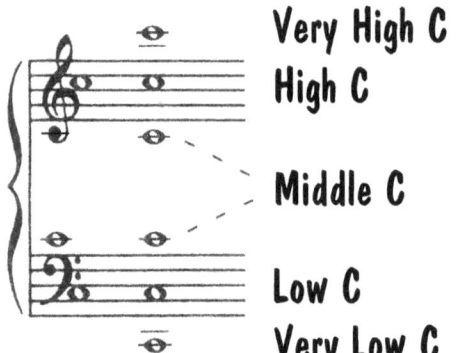

Very High C
High C
Middle C
Low C
Very Low C

Colour Coding instructions for the Signpost Notes are available at margaretbrandman.com

HOW WELL DO YOU KNOW YOUR Cs?

On which space is the Treble Clef High C written? ....

On which space is the Bass Clef Low C written? ....

How many leger lines above the Treble Staff are needed for Very High C? ....

How many leger lines below the Bass Staff are needed for Very Low C? ....

Where is Middle C located in the Treble Staff? ....

Where is Middle C located in the Bass Staff? ....

1) Copy the six Signpost Cs

2) Copy the Brace and Line, Treble Clef and Bass Clef, and the Signpost Cs two times on the staves below.

1)   2)

3) Write in the second note to match the words underneath.

Step Up   SAME   Skip Up   SAME   Jump Down   Step Down   SAME   Skip Down

Jump Up   Skip Up   SAME   Step Down   Jump Down   SAME   Step Up   Jump Up

4) Draw three skips up in a row from the given notes.

✱ Sk Sk Sk   ✱ Sk Sk Sk   ✱ Sk Sk Sk   ✱ Sk Sk Sk

ANOTHER INTERVAL

Skip-Plus-One

To play a skip-plus-one: Feel a skip and go one further.

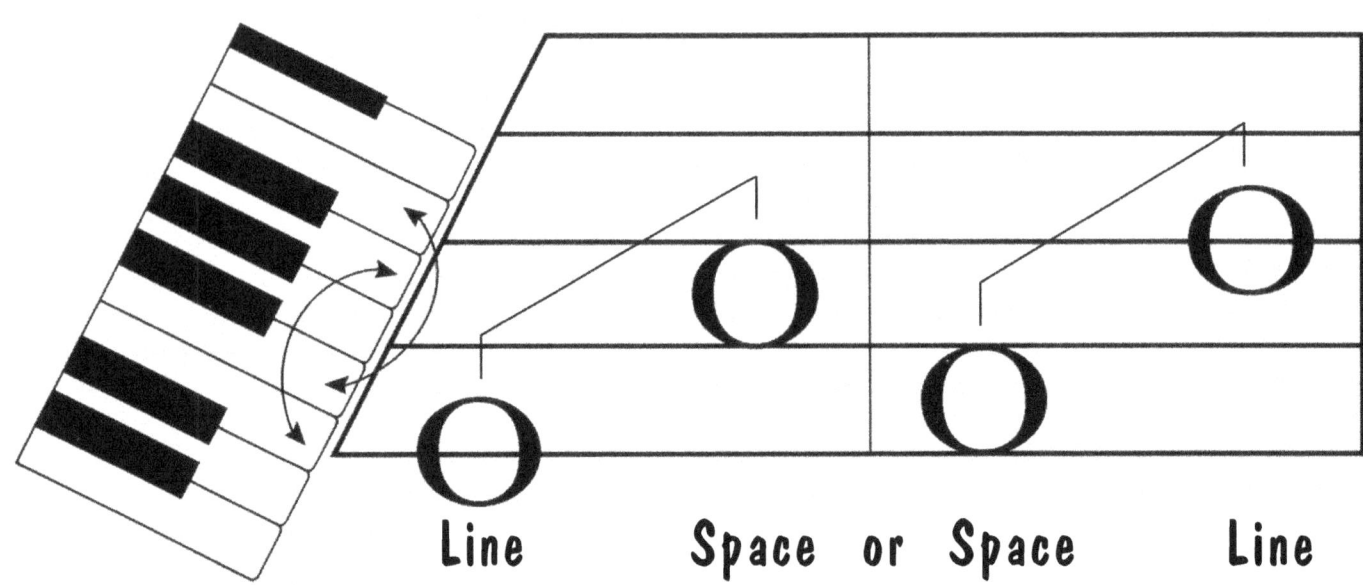

To write Skip-Plus-Ones quickly and easily, place a dot a skip away from the given note and then write the very next note past your dot.

Activities

1) Write some SKIP-PLUS-ONES going up from the given notes.

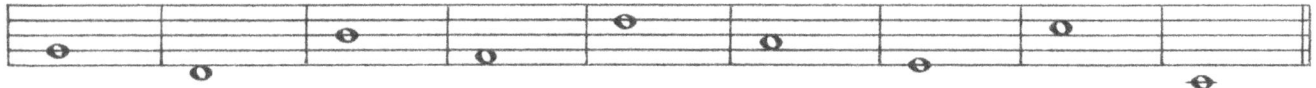

2) Write some SKIP-PLUS-ONES going down from the given notes.

WRITING INTERVALS

These five intervals can be named two ways
Simplified interval names

Traditional interval naming by size

Activities

1a) Write some Steps UP from the given notes.   **1b)** Write Steps DOWN.

e.g.

2a) Write Skips UP.   **2a)** Write Skips DOWN.

e.g.

3a) Write Skip-Plus-Ones UP.   **3b)** Write Skip-Plus-Ones DOWN.

e.g.

To write Jumps easily, place a dot for the skip and then write the next skip past your dot.
Say " Line - jump over a line - to the next line", or " space - jump over a space - to the next space".

4a) Write Jumps UP.   **4b)** Write Jumps DOWN.

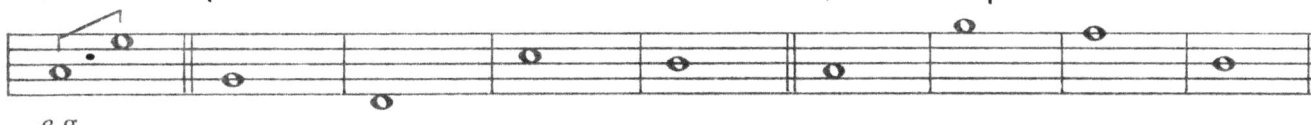

e.g.

5) Write some SAMES alongside the given notes.

RHYTHM ACTIVITIES

 Look at the top number of the time signature to see how many counts in each bar

 Colour & Clap

Colour in the boxes and clap the time values
* Hold hands together while the colour continues
* For rests - take hands apart and beat time in the air

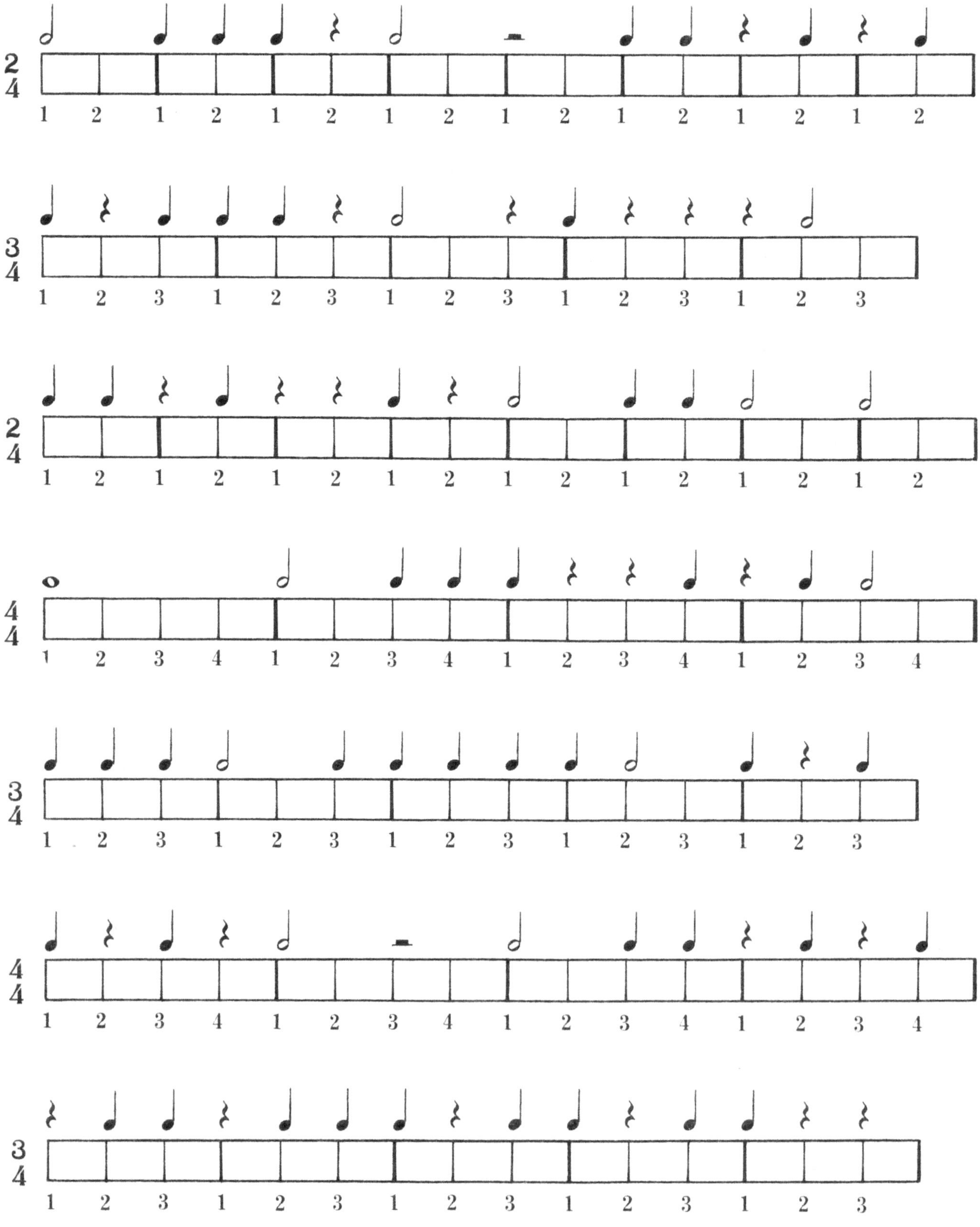

SEARCH AND RESCUE

Find the STEPS and mark them with a bracket.

(1)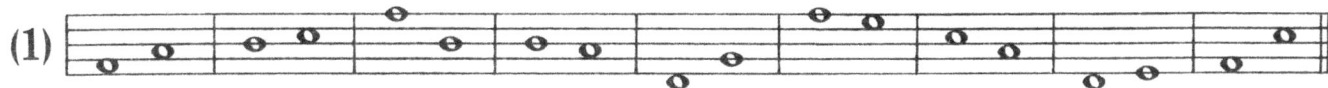

Mark the SKIPS with a bracket.

(2)

Mark the SKIP-PLUS-ONES with a bracket.

(3)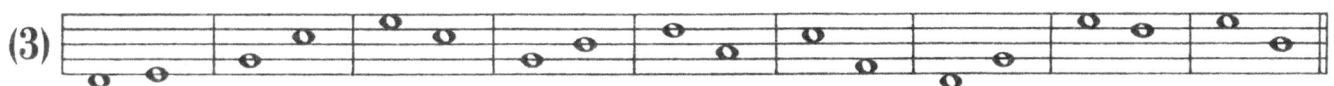

Mark the JUMPS with a bracket. Also Circle the SAMES.

(4)

Indicate whether these intervals are Steps or Skip-Plus-Ones (ST or SK+1)

(5)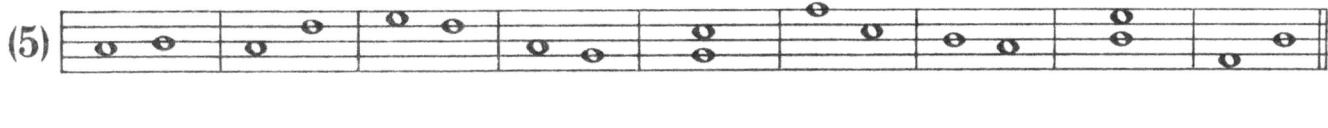

Indicate whether these intervals are Skips or Jumps (SK or J)

(6)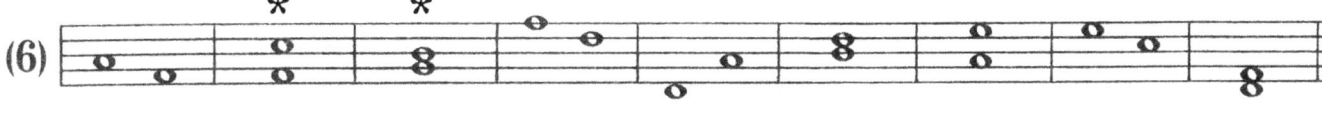

* Harmonic intervals. Both notes are sounded at the same time

INTERVAL QUIZ

1) Indicate whether the following intervals are:
   Same (S), Step (ST), Skip (SK), Skip-Plus-One (SK + 1) or Jump(J).
2) Tick the harmonic intervals with a red pencil

(1)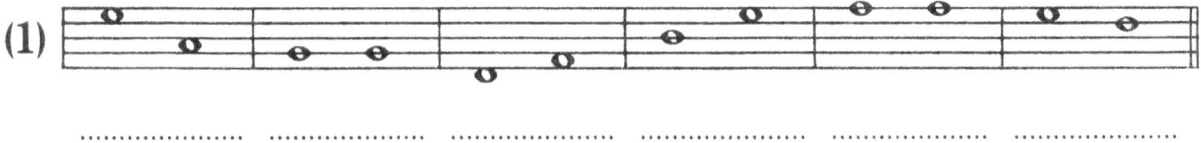

(2)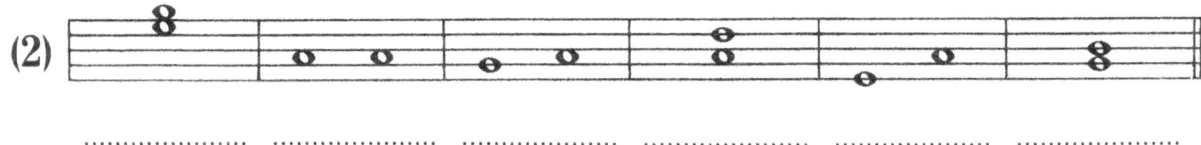

(3)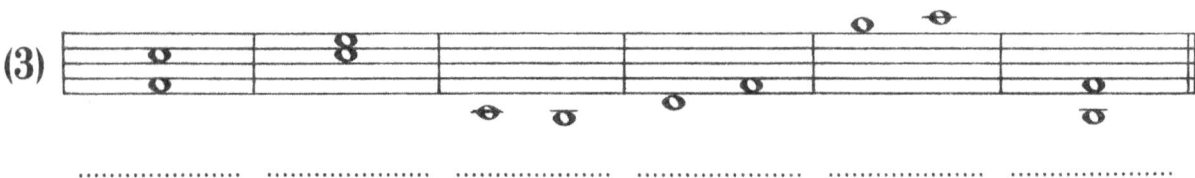

(4)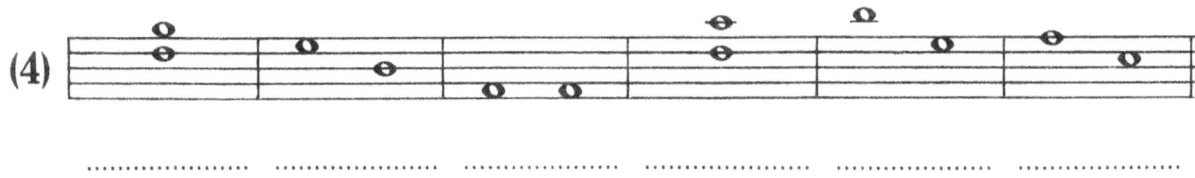

Begin Contemporary Theory Workbook 1 alongside the remaining pages of this book
to learn about the naming of notes in Treble, Bass and C Clef

RHYTHM ACTIVITIES

Colour in the boxes and clap the time values
* Hold hands together while the colour continues
* For rests - take hands apart and beat time in the air

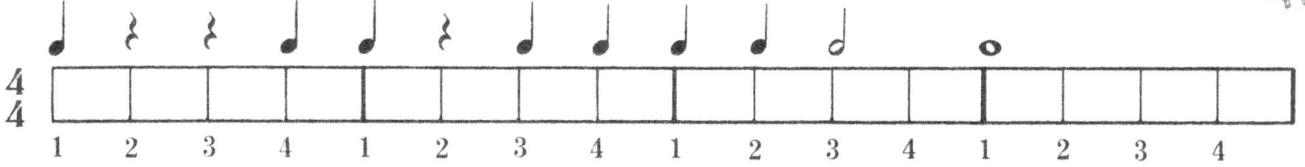

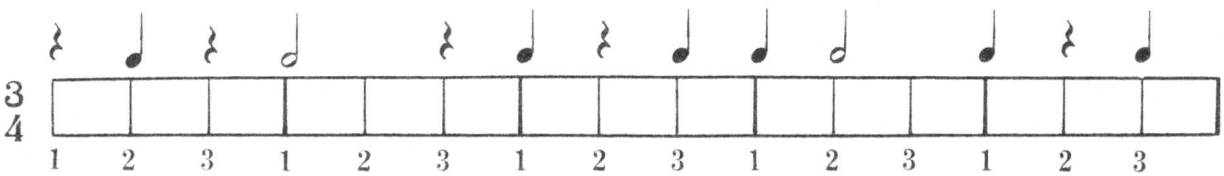

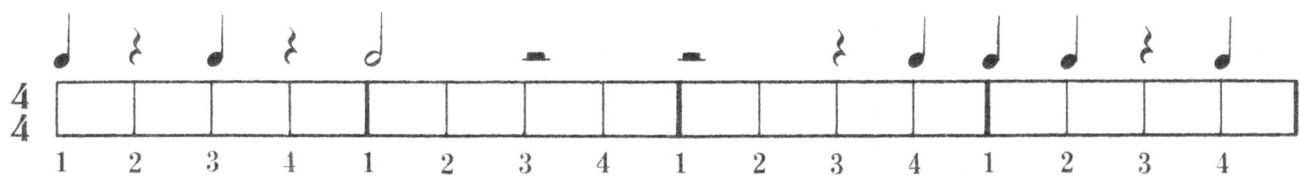

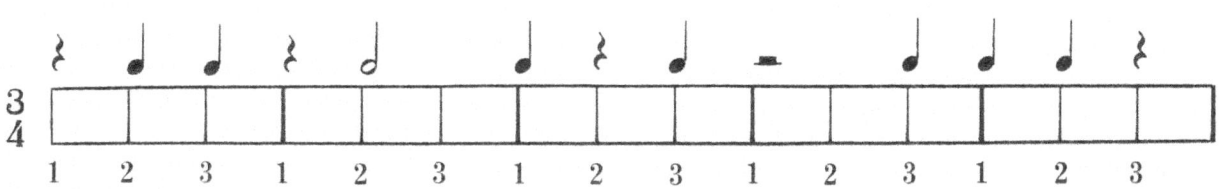

WRITING INTERVAL SETS

1) Write **four** skips UP from the given notes.

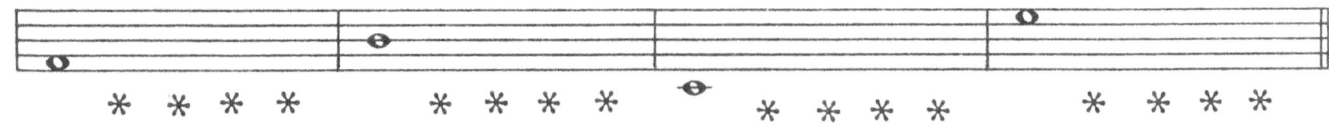

2) Write three skips DOWN from the given notes.

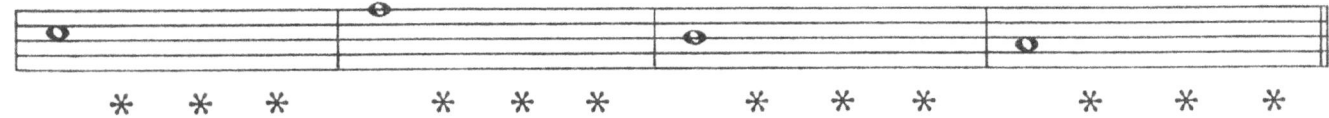

3) Write two Jumps UP from the given notes.

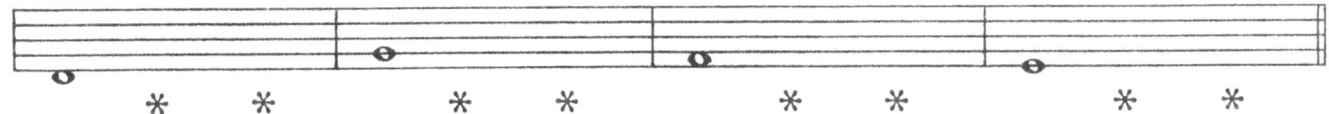

4) Write two Skip-Plus-Ones DOWN from the given notes.

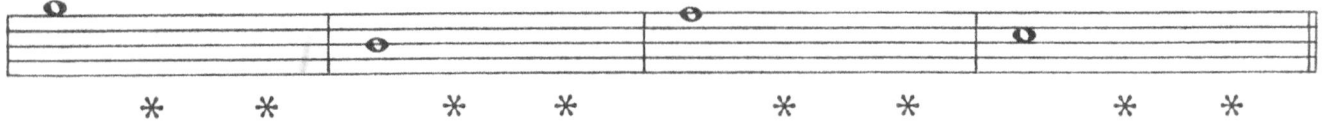

RHYTHM ACTIVITIES 25

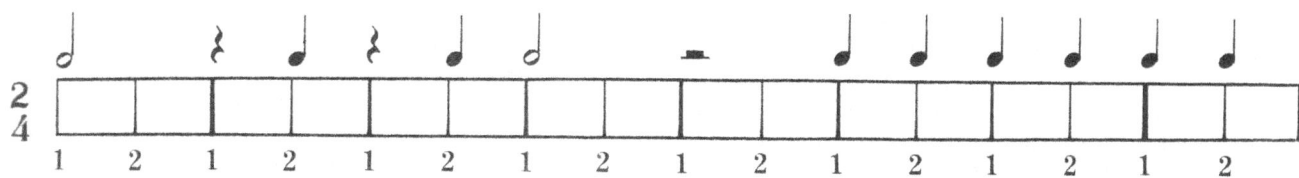

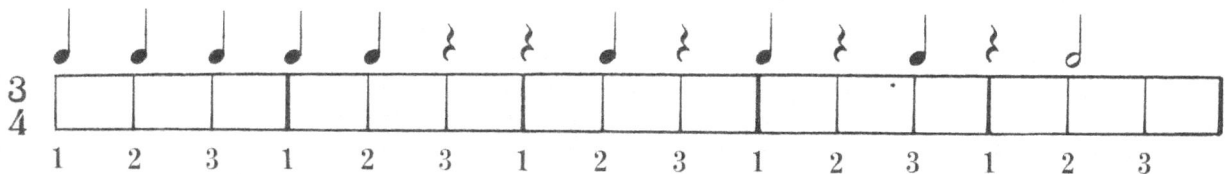

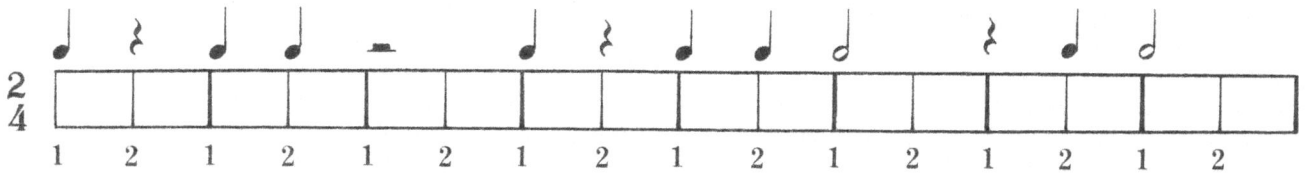

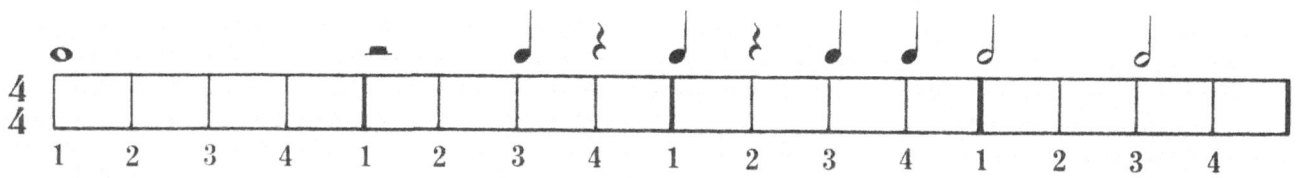

THE ROOT POSITION TRIAD

A TRIAD is a three note chord. The Root Position Triad shape is easy to see and play because it is made up of two SKIPS built on top of one another. They have a total of three notes hence the name TRI(meaning three)AD.

All three notes can be played at the same time, in which case the notes are called a **Block Triad**. The other name given to a triad is a Chord. So the shape could also be called a **Block Chord**.

If the notes are played one after another, the shape is called a **Broken Triad** or **Broken Chord**.

Example 1. BLOCK CHORDS

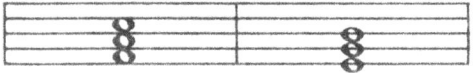

Example 2. BROKEN CHORDS

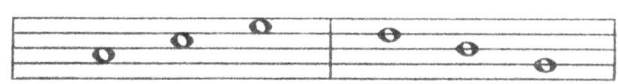

played going up   played going down

Activities

1) Write Block Triads **above** the given notes.

2) Write Block Triads **below** the given notes.

THE ROOT POSITION TRIAD

3) Indicate which of these are Block and which of these are Broken triads (chords), (use BL for Block and BR for Broken).

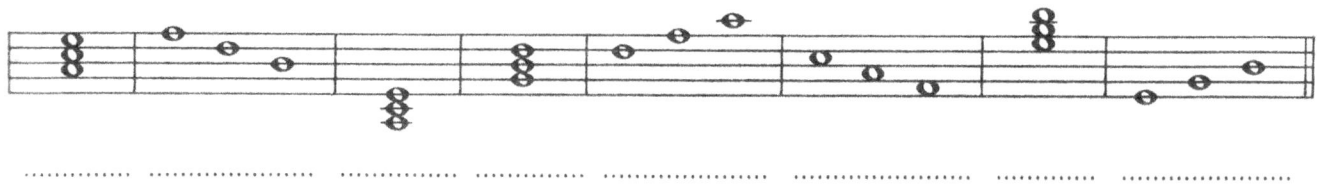

....

4) Write Broken Chords going UP from the given notes.

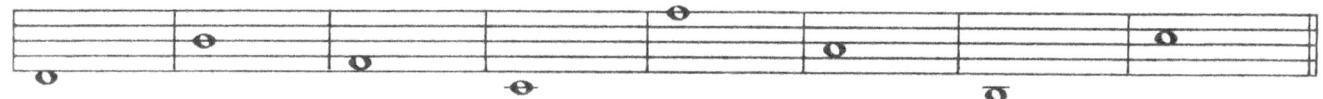

5) Write Broken Chords going DOWN from the given notes.

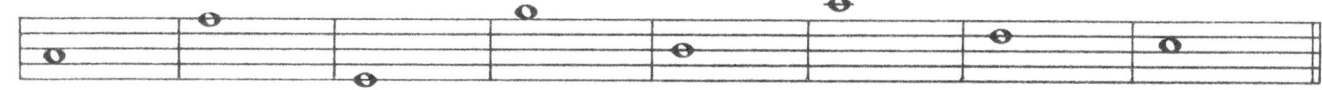

6) Circle the ROOT POSITION TRIAD shapes.

RHYTHM ACTIVITIES

Colour & Clap

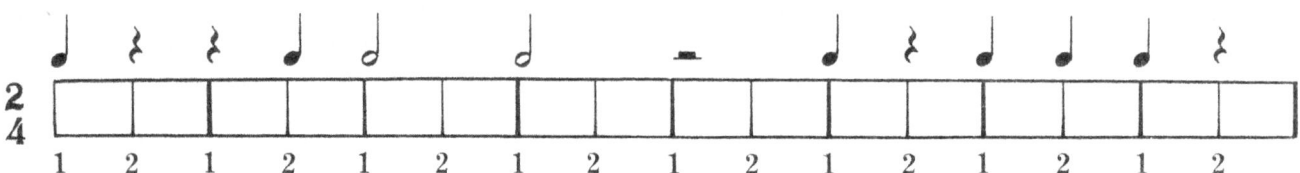

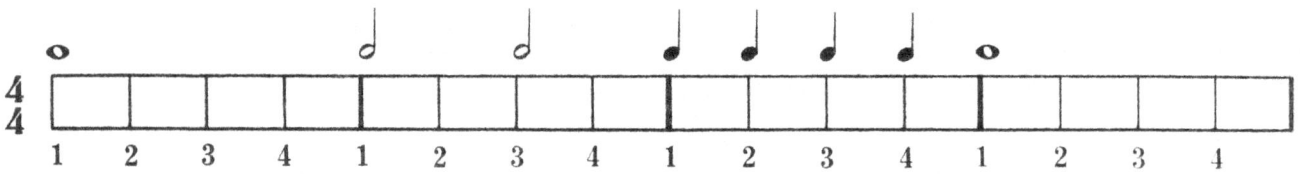

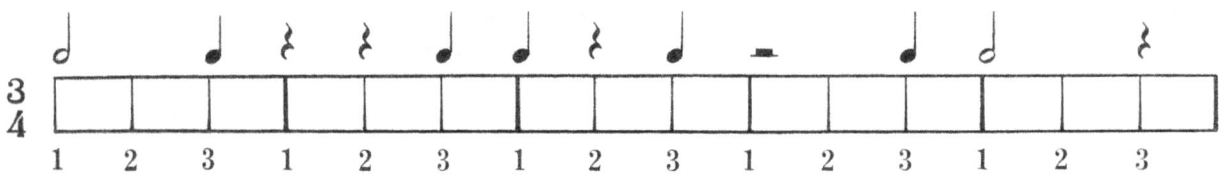

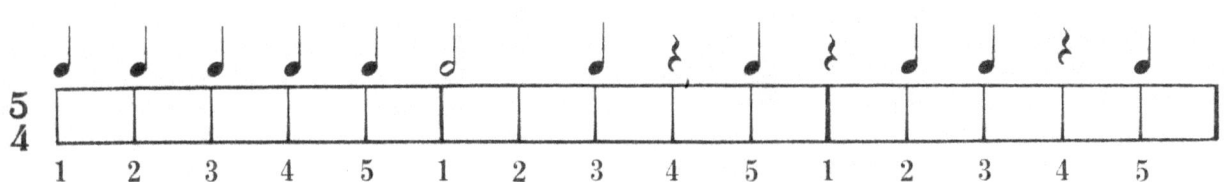

Musical examples: 'Take Five' performed by the Dave Brubeck Quartet
'Everything's All Right' from Jesus Christ Superstar
'Spider On The Mirror' and 'No. 5 is Alive' from Twelve Timely Pieces (Brandman)

LEGER LINES (29)

Leger Lines are the extra lines added to the staff, either above or below.
Intervals written on Leger Lines look exactly the same as those written on the staff.

For Example:

Activities

1) Write Steps DOWN from the given notes. Provide your own Leger Lines, using a ruler.

2) Write Skips UP from the given notes. Provide your own Leger Lines, using a ruler.

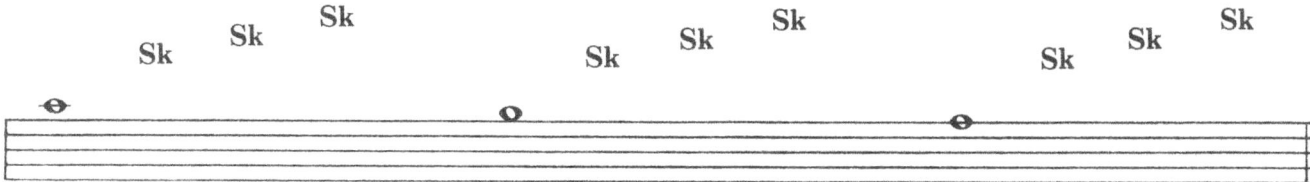

3) Identify the following intervals.

RHYTHM ACTIVITIES - ODD TIMES

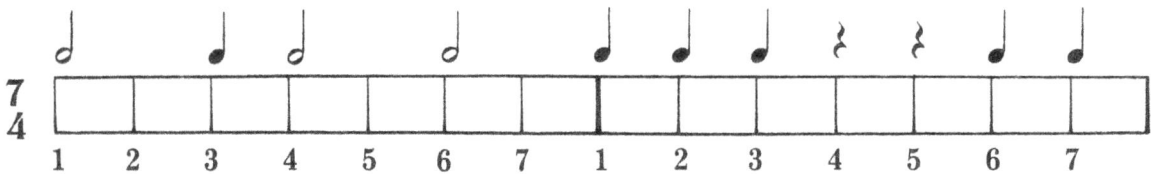

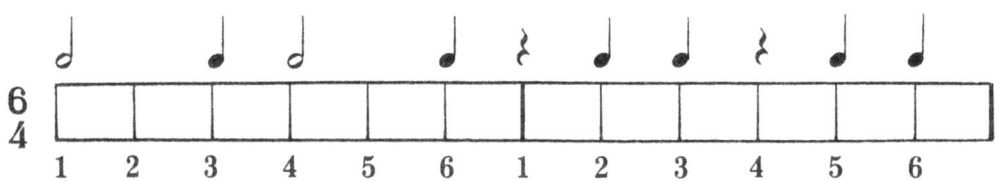

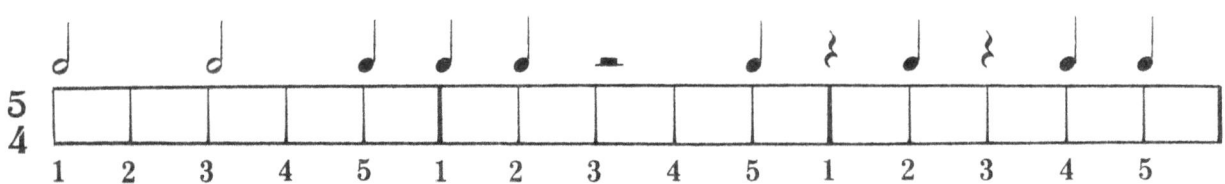

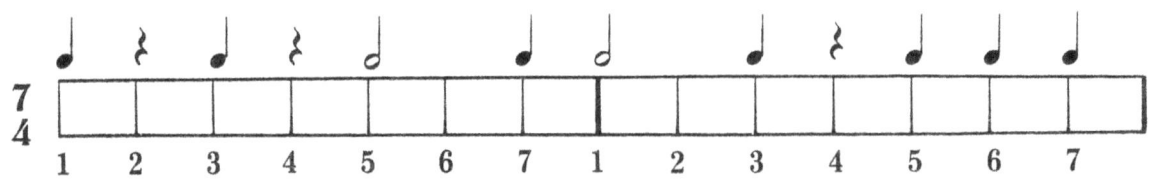

Refer to Twelve Timely Pieces (Brandman) for tunes written in all these time signatures.

STEMS

If the note is written on the Middle line, its stem can go either up or down.

If the note head is written lower than the Middle line, then the stem must go UP on the Right Hand side of the note-head.

for example:

If the note head is written higher than the Middle line, then the stem must go DOWN on the Left Hand side of the note-head.

for example:

Activities

1) Add stems to these note-heads to make them into two-count notes (Minims)

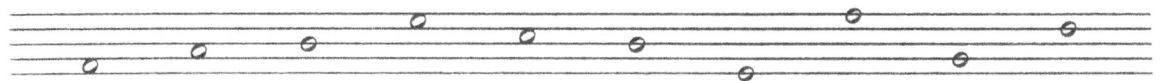

2) Add stems to these note-heads to make them into Minims. Then fill each note-head in so that the notes become one-count notes (Crotchets)

PITCH CHART AND SIGNPOST Cs

Figure 1 shows the SIGN-POST notes and all the notes between them. It also gives the hand positions that can be used to play these notes, shown by the brackets.

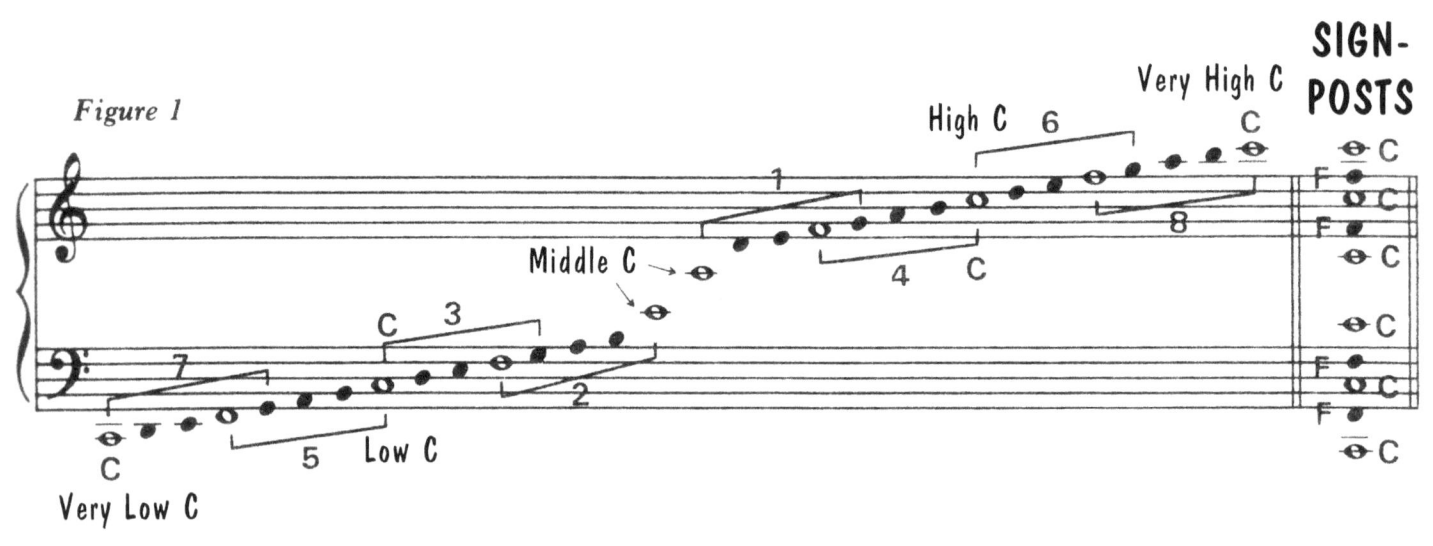

1) Copy the Signpost Cs in their memory positions.

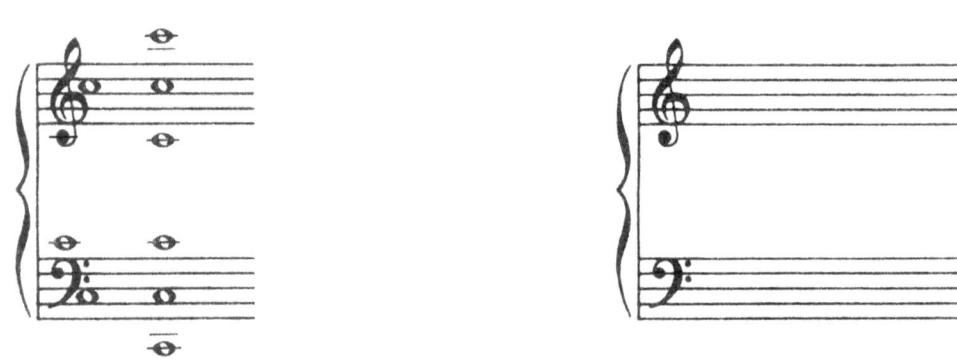

2) Copy the Brace and Line, Treble Clef and Bass Clef, and the Signpost Cs two times on the staves below.

(1)

(2)

WRITING MUSIC WITH WHOLE NOTES

REMEMBER: S stands for SAME, St stands for STEP, Sk stands for SKIP,
Sk+1 stands for SKIP-PLUS-ONE, and J stands for JUMP.

1) Using Four-Count notes (Semibreves/Whole notes) write the Intervals asked for.
   Start on MIDDLE C. The arrows tell you if the notes should go up or down.

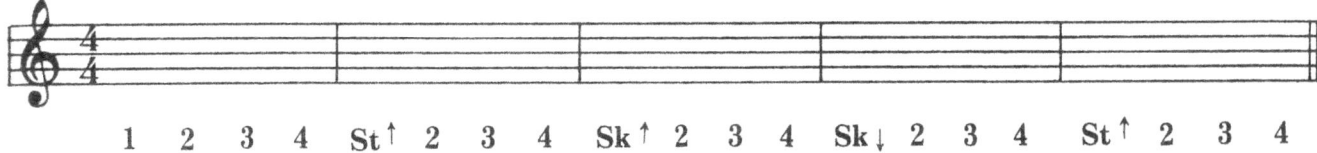

1 2 3 4   St↑ 2 3 4   Sk↑ 2 3 4   Sk↓ 2 3 4   St↑ 2 3 4

2) Using Whole Notes write the Intervals asked for, starting on MIDDLE C.

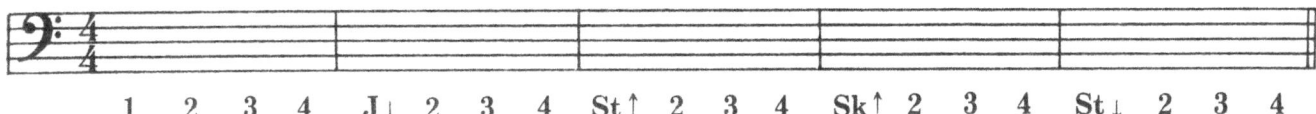

1 2 3 4   J↓ 2 3 4   St↑ 2 3 4   Sk↑ 2 3 4   St↓ 2 3 4

3) Using Whole Notes write the Intervals asked for, starting on HIGH C.

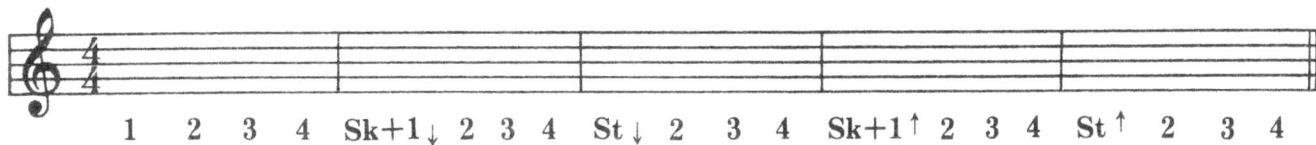

1 2 3 4   Sk+1↓ 2 3 4   St↓ 2 3 4   Sk+1↑ 2 3 4   St↑ 2 3 4

4) Using Whole Notes write the Intervals asked for, starting on LOW C.

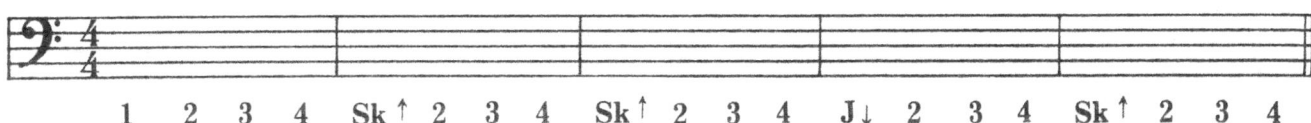

1 2 3 4   Sk↑ 2 3 4   Sk↑ 2 3 4   J↓ 2 3 4   Sk↑ 2 3 4

WRITING MUSIC WITH HALF NOTES

5) Using Two count Notes (Minims/Half notes) write the Intervals asked for, starting on HIGH C.

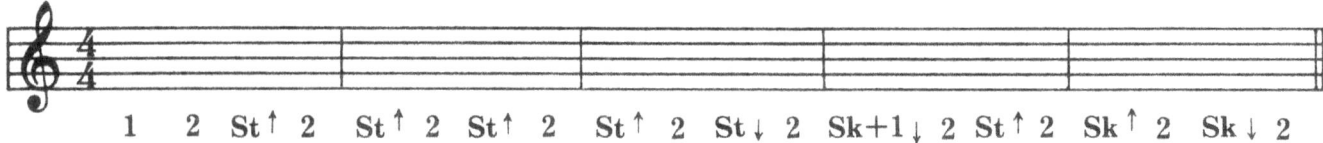

1   2   St↑ 2   St↑ 2   St↑ 2   St↑ 2   St↓ 2   Sk+1↓ 2   St↑ 2   Sk↑ 2   Sk↓ 2

6) Using Half Notes, write the Intervals asked for, starting on LOW C.

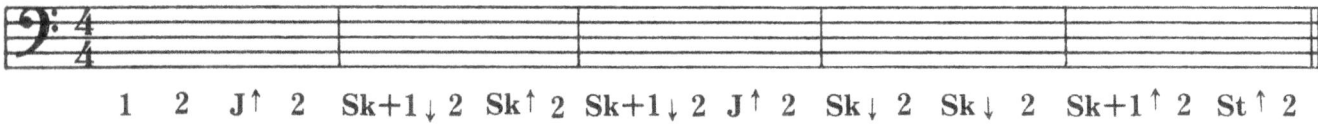

1   2   J↑ 2   Sk+1↓ 2   Sk↑ 2   Sk+1↓ 2   J↑ 2   Sk↓ 2   Sk↓ 2   Sk+1↑ 2   St↑ 2

7) Using Half Notes, write the Intervals asked for, starting on VERY HIGH C.

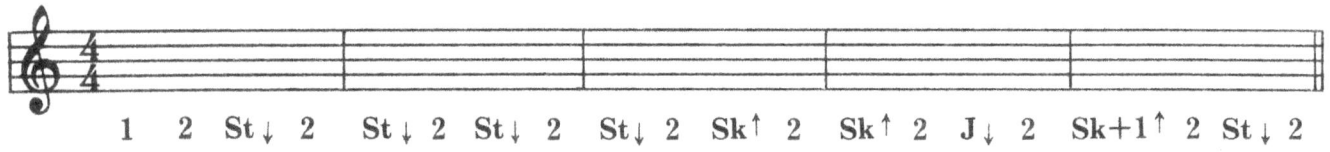

1   2   St↓ 2   St↓ 2   St↓ 2   St↓ 2   Sk↑ 2   Sk↑ 2   J↓ 2   Sk+1↑ 2   St↓ 2

8) Using Half Notes, write the Intervals asked for, starting on VERY LOW C.

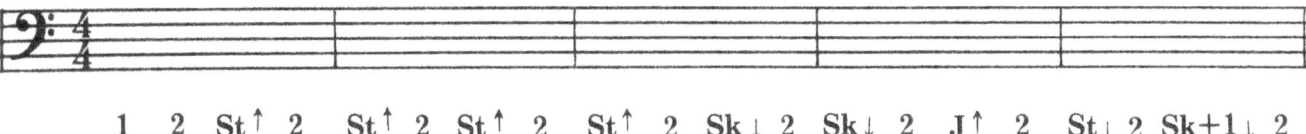

1   2   St↑ 2   St↑ 2   St↑ 2   St↑ 2   Sk↓ 2   Sk↓ 2   J↑ 2   St↓ 2   Sk+1↓ 2

WRITING MUSIC WITH QUARTER NOTES

9) Using One-Count notes, (Crotchets/Quarter notes) write the Intervals asked for, starting on MIDDLE C.

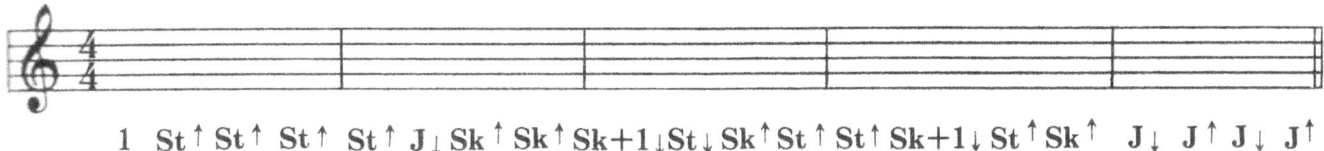

1   St↑ St↑ St↑ St↑ J↓ Sk↑ Sk↑ Sk+1↓ St↓ Sk↑ St↑ St↑ Sk+1↓ St↑ Sk↑   J↓ J↑ J↓ J↑

10) Using Quarter Notes, write the Intervals asked for, starting on MIDDLE C.
    (Don't forget that S stands for SAME)

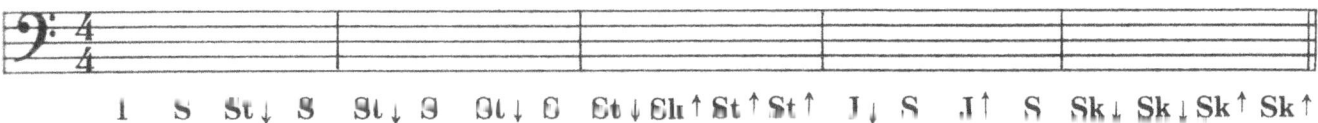

1   S St↓ S St↓ S St↓ S St↓ St↑ St↑ St↑   J↓ S J↑ S   Sk↓ Sk↓ Sk↑ Sk↑

11) Using Quarter Notes, write the Intervals asked for, starting on HIGH C.

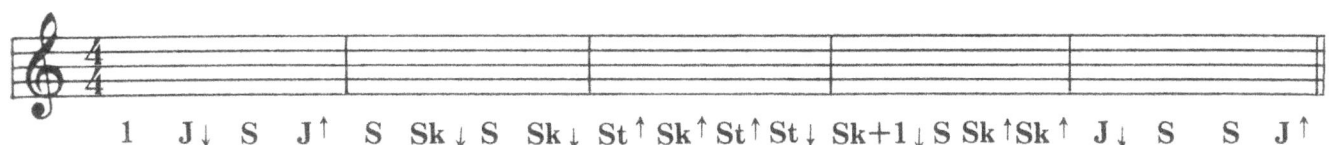

1   J↓ S J↑ S Sk↓ S Sk↓ St↑ Sk↑ St↑ St↓ Sk+1↓ S Sk↑ Sk↑   J↓ S S J↑

12) Using Quarter Notes, write the Intervals asked for, starting on LOW C.

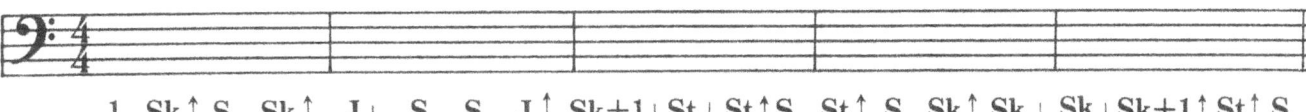

1   Sk↑ S Sk↑ J↓ S S J↑ Sk+1↓ St↓ St↑ S   St↑ S Sk↑ Sk↓ Sk↓ Sk+1↑ St↑ S

LARGER INTERVALS

Sixths

* The interval of a Sixth is one step further than a jump or 5th.
* To play one on a keyboard, stretch the fifth finger or the thumb one note beyond the hand position to reach it.
* The Sixth looks like a larger version of the Skip-Plus-One, written from a line note to a space note or vice-versa.
* Sixths have a very pleasant or Consonant sound.

6th

Sevenths

* The interval of a Seventh looks like a larger version of the Jump or Fifth.
* Sevenths are always written from line note to line note, or space note to space note.
* Sevenths have a harsh and clashy or Dissonant sound.

7th

Octaves (8ves)

* The interval of an Octave (8ve) is as far as most people can comfortably span on a keyboard.
* Like the sixth, it is always written from line to space or vice-versa.
* The letter names of the notes an octave apart are the same.
* Octaves have a pleasant but open and bare sound. They one of the Perfect Intervals.

8ve

ACTIVITIES

To write sixths more easily, place a dot where the Jump or Fifth would be and then write the note a step beyond the dot.

1) Write the SIXTHS above the given notes

2) Write the SIXTHS below the given notes

To write sevenths more easily, place a dot for Jump and then write the note a skip further away.

3) Write the SEVENTHS above the given notes

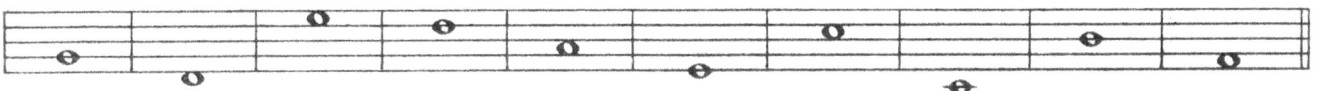

4) Write the SEVENTHS below the given notes

To write Octaves more easily, place a dot where the Seventh would be and then write the note a step beyond the dot.

5) Write OCTAVES (8ths) above the given notes

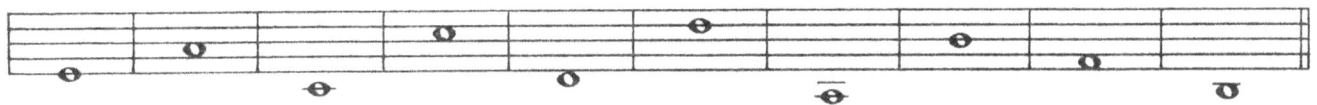

6) Write OCTAVES (8ths) below the given notes

Refer to Set Two of the Contemporary Aural Course to get to know the sounds of these three intervals.

INTERVAL OVERVIEW - UNISON TO OCTAVE

All the Intervals up to an Octave.

Compare these Intervals.

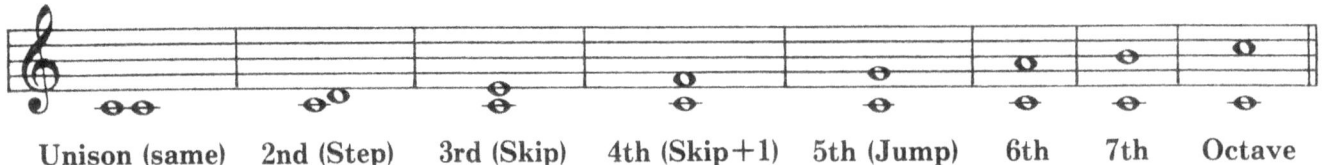

Unison (same)　2nd (Step)　3rd (Skip)　4th (Skip+1)　5th (Jump)　6th　7th　Octave

A The Members of the SKIP Family.

Space to Space　　　or Line to Line

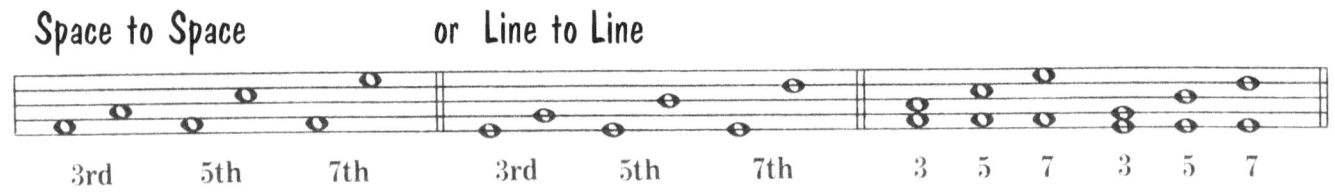

3rd　5th　7th　　3rd　5th　7th　　3　5　7　3　5　7

B The Members of the STEP Family.

Space to Line　　　or Line to Space

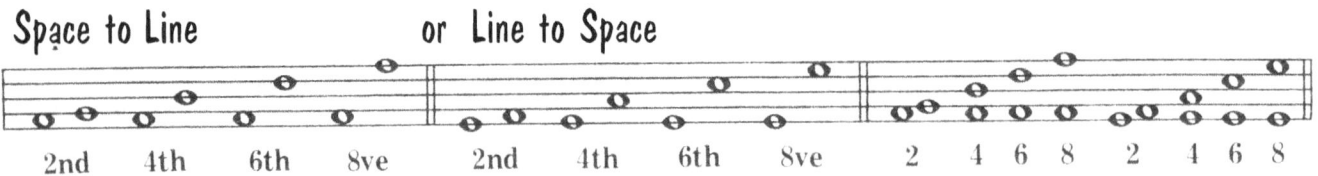

2nd　4th　6th　8ve　　2nd　4th　6th　8ve　　2　4　6　8　2　4　6　8

For more information on interval qualities (Perfect, Major and Minor), refer to Book 2 of this Contemporary Theory Workbook series.

INTERVAL FAMILY QUIZ

1) Indicate to which family these melodic intervals belong (A or B)* and name them

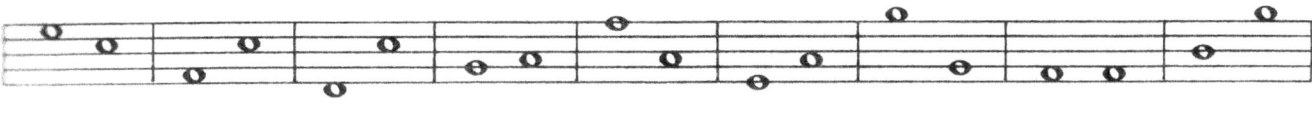

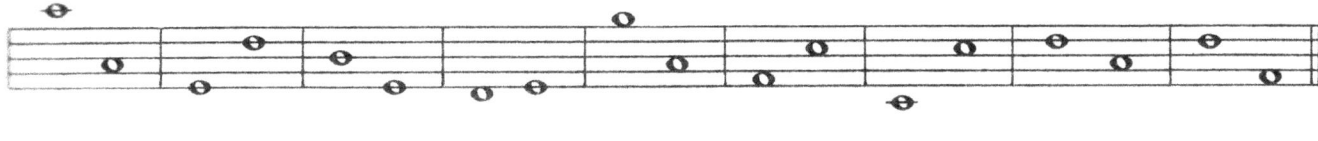

* Use Red for A and Blue for B

2) Indicate the family and size of these melodic and harmonic intervals

3) Name the following intervals

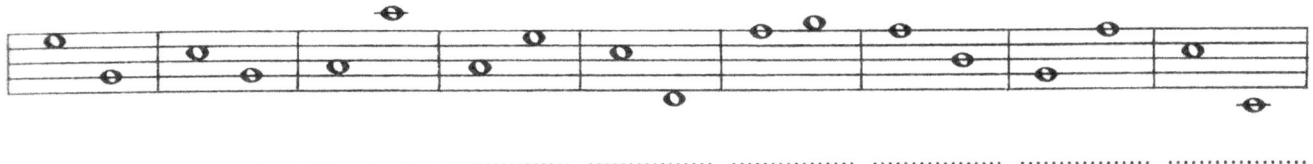

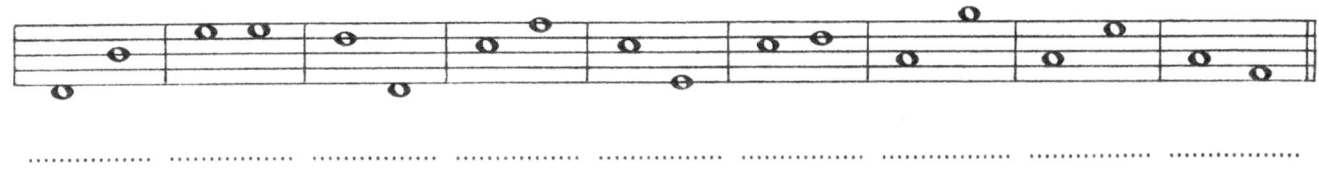

SPEED MUSIC READING QUIZ

Show the interval family to which each interval on this page belongs, by underlining each one in red or blue.

1) Write the intervals asked for **above** the given notes.

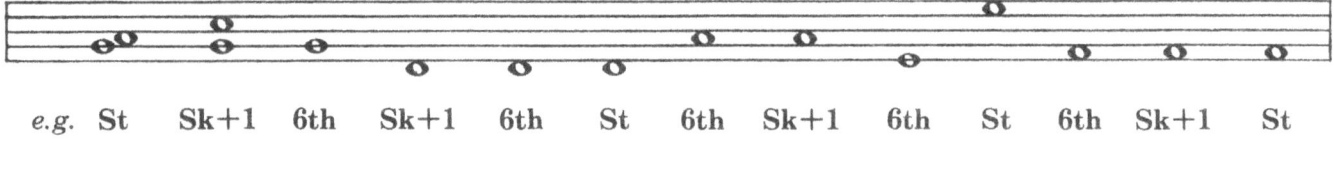

e.g. St   Sk+1   6th   Sk+1   6th   St   6th   Sk+1   6th   St   6th   Sk+1   St

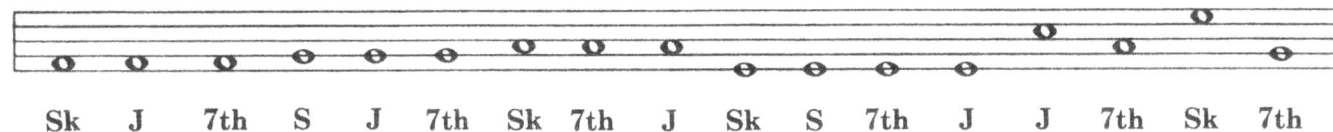

Sk   J   7th   S   J   7th   Sk   7th   J   Sk   S   7th   J   J   7th   Sk   7th

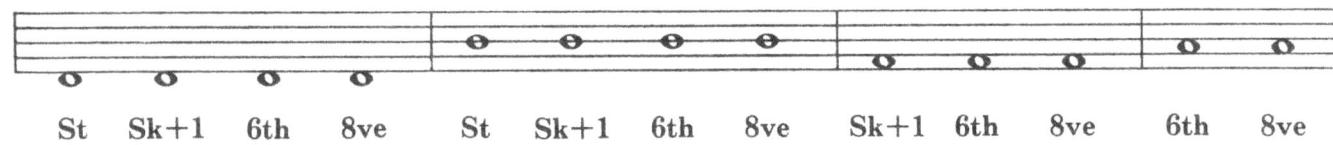

St   Sk+1   6th   8ve   St   Sk+1   6th   8ve   Sk+1   6th   8ve   6th   8ve

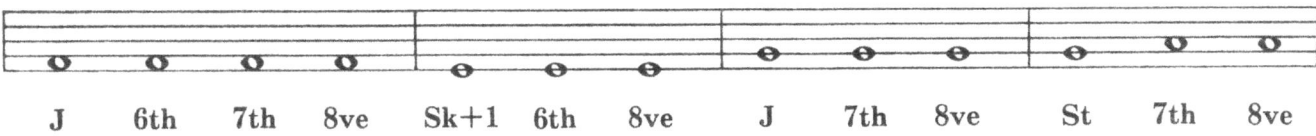

J   6th   7th   8ve   Sk+1   6th   8ve   J   7th   8ve   St   7th   8ve

2) Write the intervals asked for **below** the given notes.

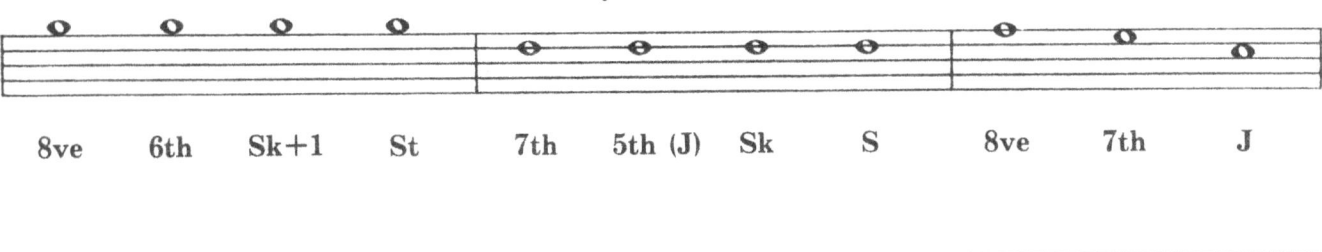

8ve   6th   Sk+1   St   7th   5th (J)   Sk   S   8ve   7th   J

J   6th   8ve   5th   7th   Sk+1   6th   Sk   5th   S   Sk+1   8ve   J

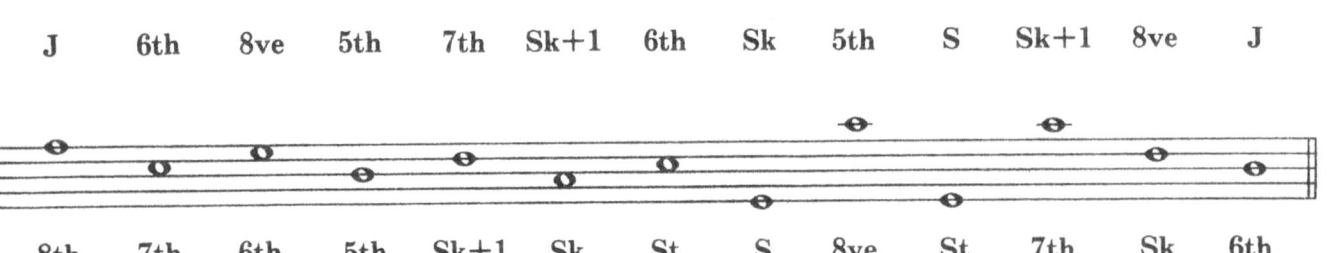

8th   7th   6th   5th   Sk+1   Sk   St   S   8ve   St   7th   Sk   6th

www.ingramcontent.com/pod-product-compliance
Lightning Source LLC
Chambersburg PA
CBHW080855090426
42734CB00013B/2997